ques

The Private CARY GRANT

The Private
CARY
GRANT

WILLIAM CURRIE McINTOSH
AND WILLIAM WEAVER

SIDGWICK & JACKSON
LONDON

First published in 1983 in Great Britain
by Sidgwick and Jackson Limited

This softcover edition
first published in1987

ISBN 0–283–99511–4

Phototypeset by Falcon Graphic Art Ltd
Wallington, Surrey
Printed in Great Britain by
R.J.Acford, Chichester, Sussex
for Sidgwick and Jackson Limited
1 Tavistock Chambers, Bloomsbury Way
London WC1A 2SG

Contents

Acknowledgements

The authors wish to extend their gratitude to the following individuals: Caroline Moorehead, Patrick Seale, Paul Richard Smith, F. Michael Martin, Hampton J. Rector, David Weaver, Richard Schwartz, E.V. Burt, Elizabeth Reich, Andrew J. McNulty, and William Currie McIntosh II.

The Private CARY GRANT

1

The Chancy Business
of a Special Oscar

The seventh of April, a Thursday, was the day fixed for Hollywood's 1970 Academy Awards. The occasion, in a city renowned for the splendour and exuberance of its theatrical presentations, was to be made still more splendid by the appearance on stage of an actor, remarkably, never before so honoured: Cary Grant. For the sixty-six-year-old actor, most loved of all Hollywood's leading men, veteran of seventy-two feature films, and nominated for his performance in two of them, had never actually won an Oscar. To make amends, the movie world, long unhappy at this oversight, were preparing to acclaim him in style. Frank Sinatra was to present him with the most prestigious of the Academy's prizes: the Special Oscar, awarded only to the greatest – and the most neglected – of the Hollywood stars.

There was only one flaw in the otherwise perfect planning of the evening. Cary Grant refused to reveal whether or not he would be attending. In the weeks following the Academy's announcement about the Special Oscar, Grant simply shut himself up in his house in Beverly Hills, deliberating and procrastinating. Some days he let it be understood that he would be coming, provided that the arrangements for his arrival and departure could be stage-managed precisely as he asked. Others, he refused to answer the telephone, or, if reached by an increasingly perturbed Academy official, managed to sound extremely doubtful about the whole occasion.

As the winter days passed, and April grew nearer, so those in the Academy charged with orchestrating the evening grew desperate:

the sequence of a presentation traditionally includes clips from the major films of the actor being honoured, and much time and care is devoted to the selection and juxtaposition of the items used. What was more, since the celebration is invariably televised, split-second timing is crucial. Long before the day in question, the organizers have to know the exact length of the speech of acceptance. Finally, early in March, Gregory Peck, president of the Academy, took to phoning Grant himself, reasoning with him, begging him to make some kind of decision, either way.

Nothing happened. Grant, apparently unmoved, declined to commit himself. He sat on, in silence, brooding by his pool in the early spring sunshine. Eventually he did make one concession. He allowed his young secretary, Bill Weaver, to drive to the Music Center in Los Angeles, where the Awards were to be presented, to examine the building, establish the number and layout of its exits and entrances, and calculate the minutes it would take from street level to his dressing room and back.

By 1970 Cary Grant, the most genial and suave of all Hollywood's male leads for more than three decades, had acquired something of a reputation as a recluse. He was rarely seen in public, refused most social engagements, and ate all his meals at home. No one was ever invited to his house. Friends talked about Howard Hughes and reminded each other how much Grant had always admired him.

But this was something different. Had the organizers but known, there was an extremely simple explanation for this bout of seemingly irrational prevarication. A one-time call-girl named Cynthia Bouron had just told Grant that she was going to sue him for the paternity of her new baby. And what better place to broadcast her intentions, and thereby secure lavish financial settlements and not a little publicity, than on the stage of the Los Angeles Music Center, in front of 3,000 invited Hollywood celebrities, on live, coast-to-coast, prime-time television?

It would have been wrong to take Cynthia Bouron's threats too lightly. Her past behaviour had shown that she was more than capable of such a gesture. She was a short, volatile girl in her late twenties, with the kind of changeable looks that could make her appear sultry and pouting one day, pert and pixie-like the next, rather frumpish on a third. People who knew her spoke of her disparagingly as a 'Tijuana hooker', a girl so affected by her experiences that she had become like the border village between Mexico and California whose slum-like decrepitness had made its name a byword on the West Coast. What was more, she had a highly dubious marriage behind her, to a man who had been caught up in a triangular suicide-murder case involving one of Mickey Rooney's wives. Cary Grant, who had been introduced to her by friends in Los Angeles, had taken her out on a couple of evenings, then brought her back to his house off Benedict Canyon to spend the night. Their affair – though such brief dates hardly constituted an 'affair' – had been over for many months.

Grant had first had an intimation of what was to come not long before Gregory Peck wrote to give him the news about the Award. One afternoon a car had wound its way up the steep and generally deserted road leading to the one-storey house he liked to call North African, jutting out vertiginously over the canyon, and parked by the white wooden gates. From it had alighted Cynthia Bouron, clutching a newly born baby, heavily swaddled in shawls and crying loudly. From the other side of the fence Bill Weaver, sent to the gate to handle the matter, told her that on no account was anyone going to let her in. 'Very well,' she replied, 'I'll wait.' With which, still clasping the baby, she returned to her car.

When night fell the local police, alerted on their regular rounds of the district by the presence of an unfamiliar parked car, offered to move her on. Grant, when consulted, refused. He and Bill Weaver had agreed that the best way to avoid publicity was to pretend that nothing was happening.

The siege went on. The still silence of the valley, with its few exotic film stars' houses perched like eyries around the canyon, was repeatedly broken throughout the night by howls of rage, as Cynthia Bouron bawled obscenities in the direction of the apparently sleeping household. From his bedroom near the front door, Bill Weaver could hear the gate being rattled.

15

The matter of the threatened paternity suit would have been serious enough without its coming just as Hollywood finally made up its mind to confer on Grant the most public of its public awards. Under Californian law, supposed fathers are presumed guilty until cleared by the courts, and must bear all costs to do with the pregnancy and birth of a baby until the case is heard.

And so, as the days passed, and 7 April crept even closer, so Grant grew more agitated. Pacing up and down the corridors of his house, he spent his time alternating between drafting speeches of grateful acceptance for the Oscar, discussing them sentence by sentence with Bill Weaver, and concocting ever more fantastic and ludicrous jokes about Cynthia Bouron. 'I know what *really* happened,' he said one morning, laughing, to Weaver. He then explained how it was now obvious to him that Cynthia had performed fellatio on him one night after he had fallen asleep, hurried home with the semen still in her mouth, and asked her doctor friend, in whose house she lived, to inject it into her.

Eventually 7 April arrived, with still no mention of Grant's name as recipient of the Special Oscar in the newspapers, which carried prominent photographs of the other film people due to receive awards that same night. In the morning Gregory Peck rang. Would Grant at least divulge, he asked in a somewhat exasperated tone, whether he actually intended to turn up? Grant, cornered, capitulated. He would come, he said, provided that his presence was kept a secret until the very last moment; and then he told Gregory Peck about the dilemma that he was in. Peck was sympathetic.

The presentation, which under other circumstances might have pleased Grant more than any other honour received during his entire life, as a visible gesture of esteem from the world he had chosen to enter some forty years before, turned instead into a bad parody of a Restoration comedy. It might, in fact, have come straight from the cutting-room floor of one of the many comic movies in which Grant had starred. Weaver drove Grant's Rolls-Royce into a back alley behind the Music Center and stopped beside a little-used entrance. Here, the furtive prize winner was greeted by

Gregory Peck in person, rather than the more usual pageboy, who ushered him swiftly along back corridors and tradesmen's entrances to the dressing room which had been allocated to him. In it, Grant found Frank Sinatra rehearsing with his guitarist. The four men waited, Grant and Weaver in apprehensive silence, until the cue was given for them all to appear on stage.

Bill Weaver had been working for Grant for nearly five years. Better than anyone, he knew precisely how desperately Grant hated making speeches. Now, fearing that the threat of a nationwide televised scandal might terrorize him into total silence, he had prudently typed a second copy of the acceptance speech on to cards, ready to pass over in case Grant dropped the first set. Following Grant up on the stage as far as he possibly could without appearing conspicuous, he positioned himself behind a bank of lights and peered about him.

Grant spoke for just over ten minutes. Normally jovial, if not relaxed, he appeared rattled, glancing frequently around him. Few members of the audience seemed to notice anything unusual; but to close friends, like William McIntosh, a business associate, the actor had never looked so tense and miserable. From behind him, Weaver, out of the beam of the footlights, searched the packed audience for any sign of imminent explosion. As the minutes passed and no scene occurred, Grant calmed down.

Before the event, Grant and Weaver had agreed to make their getaway as soon as the actual presentation was over. Even if, by some merciful piece of luck, Cynthia Bouron had not managed to get him subpoenaed on prime-time, nationwide television, her lawyers would now know precisely where to find him. And so, as Mrs Sam Goldwyn and Sammy Davis Jr leapt to their feet to lead the standing ovation, Grant began backing away towards the exit, leaving 3,000 exhilarated onlookers perplexed at such bashfulness.

Once out in the corridor, Grant sped off down the passage in the direction of the parked Rolls, with Weaver trotting at his side. The two men were just congratulating themselves on a successfully accomplished foray into the public world when quickening footsteps sounded out in the corridor behind them. They panicked.

Breaking into a run, they hurtled off down a dimly lit passage, only to hear the footsteps break into a run behind them. Their pursuer seemed to be catching up on them. It was now becoming clear that Grant was not going to get away unchallenged. He stopped, resigned himself to the indignity of having a writ served in the darkened bowels of an immense theatre complex, and turned to face the coming footsteps. Out of the twilight, panting hard, emerged Gregory Peck, clasping in his hand a gold figure perched on a pedestal. It was the Special Oscar. In his haste to get away, Grant had forgotten to pick it up.

Though Cynthia Bouron had indeed lost a perfect opportunity to humiliate him, she didn't abandon her campaign. A date was set for the court hearing and Grant was forced to undergo tests to establish his blood group as well as his sperm count. Meanwhile, he took counter-measures of his own. Through Stanley Fox, his attorney, he employed a discreet detective to look into Cynthia Bouron's life, in the hope that there might be some particle of evidence to prove that the baby was in fact not his. In this he was remarkably fortunate. Apart from an exceedingly squalid assortment of past lovers, the detective was unable to establish anything of importance until he hit on the idea of getting his girlfriend to apply for a job as maid in the house in which Cynthia Bouron was living. The baby, when unwrapped from its many layers of clothing, turned out, unequivocally, not to be Grant's at all. It was half black.

Polaroid photographs of the child, smuggled from the house by the detective's girlfriend, as well as the results of the tests, which showed Grant to be, at that moment at least, infertile, ensured that the case was dropped as soon as it came before the court and Grant soon recovered from what had been an extremely unpleasant ordeal.

The episode of the Academy Awards is important in Grant's life. More clearly than most anecdotes, perhaps, it reveals the flaws in a character who made a career out of being flawless, a golden god who seemed to have defied even the process of ageing. The trumped-up paternity suit showed him to be as muddled, uncertain, and insecure as anyone else. Neither nicer nor nastier: simply mortal.

The timing of the presentation, too, was somewhat ironical. For by the spring of 1970, Cary Grant had been out of movies altogether for nearly four years. He had every intention of remaining that way.

2

Bristol Beginnings

Cary Grant was born Archibald Alexander Leach in a small back street in the suburbs of Bristol on the morning of 18 January 1904. There was nothing in his background or in the world of a provincial English town in the early years of the twentieth century to suggest the glorious future that lay ahead of him. More than most people, Grant seems to have left his roots behind him.

Archie's father, Elias, was a tailor's presser, a handsome, rather tall man with what his son was later to call a 'fancy' moustache. Outwardly, he was good humoured and affable; inside, wrote Grant nearly sixty years later, 'he had a sad acceptance of the life he had chosen.' Not that Elias was ever out of work, having a regular job with Todd's Clothing Factory off Portland Square. But his wife, Elsie Kingdon, a slight, appealing woman with olive skin and a deceptive air of frailty, had ambitions far beyond the means of a tailor's presser. To compensate for lack of worldly possessions she kept her only son – a first baby, another boy, had died shortly after being born – in lace and baby dresses, then in long curls, long after the boy felt it to be right.

It was not unusual in those days to keep moving house, particularly given Elias' trade and Elsie's aspirations. Archie started life at 15 Hughendon Road, a square, unpretentious, brick terrace house on what were then the outskirts of the city. Years later, Grant was to talk to Bill Weaver about the wild strawberry patches in the land behind the house which led down to open fields. Elias was a keen gardener, and alongside his vegetables he planted a charming

21

English flower garden, with fuchsias and hollyhocks, geraniums and daffodils, crocuses and lilies of the valley. From the main bough of the garden's one apple tree he hung a swing, thereby providing his son with his first terror of heights, a fear that was to persist well into Archie's acting career.

In keeping with his mother's ambitions – she believed her only son to be extremely gifted – Archie was sent off to school not at the normal age of five, but six months earlier. Bishop Road Junior School was a somewhat bleak, mock-Gothic board school, with a red tile roof and gables and the usual two entrances: one for boys and one for girls. Soon after starting there, Archie moved with his parents to 5 Seymour Avenue, another undistinguished turn-of-the-century terrace house from which he would walk each morning to school, past the Baptist Church, the little row of modest shops, the pub, the Union Hall.

It was not an unhappy childhood. Elsie was strict, but she was also loving. Archie was taught to polish his shoes until they gleamed and to raise his cap to adults. At weekends he wore an Eton collar made of linen. (For school it was celluloid.) He received sixpence a week pocket money – quite a lavish sum in those days – but was then docked the exorbitant sum of twopence for every gravy spot he made on the white Sunday tablecloth. He was a cheerful, if not particularly diligent, schoolboy, reserving his real dislike for the piano mistress who came to coach him at home, an 'unhandsome, irascible' woman as he was later to say. The Leaches were churchgoers, attending the local Episcopalian Church; Elias, though probably from a Jewish background himself, was happy to go along with his wife's Protestantism.

But there were treats, and these proved extraordinarily important in Archie's life. Both Elsie and Elias, somewhat improbably, loved the cinema. Like millions of other people all over the world, they were fast becoming addicts of this remarkable new medium, these flickering images that came stuttering up on to screens to the put-put of a generator and the cheerful melodies of an organ. Typically, they each did their film viewing in their own way. Elsie preferred the Claire Street Cinema, where the audience could sip tea graciously while watching the films. Elias, on the other hand, attended the Metropole, a large, draughty, barn-like place which smelled strongly of raincoats and galoshes. Since both parents took him along with them, Archie didn't mind where they went, but he did have a sneaking preference for his father's outings, since they included a pause at the local tobacconist to buy pipe tobacco, followed by a second pause at the shop next door to purchase a small bag of apples, either Russets or Morgan Sweets. Very occasionally there would be some round white peppermints or a bar of chocolate. It was munching these that Archie caught his first glimpse of Charlie Chaplin, Mack Swain, Roscoe Arbuckle, and Bronco Billy Anderson, the cowboy star.

Just before the war broke out Elias made one effort to bring home a larger salary. He moved, on his own, to a more important clothing firm in Southampton, some eighty miles away, his friends having presented him with an engraved watch and chain as a leaving gift. The venture proved a failure. Elias was soon back in Bristol. The period of separation for the Leaches, however, had not done anything to improve a relationship growing more distant for many years. Elsie, for all her apparent frailty and gentility, was an ambitious, embittered woman. Today, some cure for her acute unhappiness might have been found in drugs or therapy. Edwardian England had little to offer.

One afternoon Archie, aged nine, came home from school to find his mother gone. He asked anxiously for her. She had gone away for a holiday to the seaside, said his father; she was tired, she needed a rest. Elsie did not reappear. Soon the boy stopped asking for her. Twenty years were to pass before Archie learned that his mother had in fact been incarcerated in Bristol's mental hospital at a place called Fishponds. By the time someone told him, he was a star, 'known to most people of the world by sight and by name, yet not,' he was to explain, a little bitterly, 'to my mother'.

For a while, Elias and Archie continued to live much as they always had. Two female cousins who had been sharing their home in Seymour Avenue kept house for them and, if Archie missed his mother, at least he was not lonely. But then the cousins decided to

23

leave Bristol, and Archie and Elias moved to a dark three-storey house in Picton Street owned by Elias' mother, which lay a couple of miles down the hill towards the city centre. The streets were more obviously working-class than the suburbs Archie was used to, with shops below the houses and pokey, damp rooms. It was lit by gas. Archie's bedroom was at the top of the house at the back.

He was now reaching adolescence and ready to move to a secondary school. Despite earlier laziness he studied hard and won a free place at a respected local school called Fairfields Secondary, another gabled, red-brick, rather gaunt establishment a bare ten minutes' walk from Picton Street. The school gave on to a railway cutting and had a fine view over the Gloucestershire hills.

Archie was not a gregarious boy, being shy and particularly awkward in the presence of girls. But he was good-tempered and tall for his age and a popular choice for football games. That first winter he had an accident that could easily have blighted the career that now lay so near. Walking across the frozen playground after school, he was knocked to the ground by another pupil sliding on the ice. His front tooth snapped in two. Not wanting to confront his father with another bill, he sought out a free dental school and had the other half removed, leaving a vast gap between his upper front teeth. In time, the gap closed, giving him a set of regular but unevenly numbered teeth, and a smile since become legendary for its charm, but not before he had had a considerable amount of fun squirting jets of water at unfortunate passers-by.

At the end of the first spring term, Archie, who had been watching with envy as the school cadet corps busied itself with the military activities of the First World War, applied for any kind of local war work. He had barely reached his teens but, being tall for his age, and a hard-working member of his school scout pack, he was given a holiday job as a messenger boy in the Southampton docks. The sight, night after night, of the young soldiers embarking on troop ships (they gave the messenger boys little mementoes of military life in the form of regimental buttons and badges in exchange for delivering personal and illegal messages) left a deep impression on him. When, at the end of his Easter holidays, he returned to Bristol, he spent many hours haunting the docks that in those days filled the heart of the city, watching the barges unloading their cargoes and dreaming of distant lands and feats of glory. By now Archie had become extremely conscious of public duty, keeping his boy scout uniform, neatly pressed, laid out in readiness by his bed.

And now one of those rare episodes that seem to come out of an unsuspecting sky and for ever mark the destiny of the receiver befell him. Archie had not turned into a particularly promising student at Fairfields either, but he was very interested in chemistry, hanging around the classroom after lessons to talk over experiments with the part-time assistant electrician who came in to help the teacher with them.

It so happened that this electrician had just finished installing the lighting and a switchboard at the recently opened Hippodrome Theatre and, being a kindly man, he invited Archie one afternoon to come with him backstage. When the two of them got to the theatre, the matinée was in full swing. 'And that,' wrote Grant many years later, 'was when I *knew*!' The bustle of performers, jostling each other as they queued in the wings to go on stage, and the sight of so many costumes and such finery; the glare of the lights and the splendour of the immense, domed, red-and-gold plush theatre with its early art-deco, glass-stained windows and its air of ornate opulence, all acted as a sort of spell on the young boy.

From that day on Archie laid siege to the theatre. He hung around the stage door and under the electricians' feet picking up odd jobs and running errands for them. Finally, taking pity on him, his electrician friend introduced him to the manager of the nearby Empire, who agreed to let him help the men working on the arc lamps. Even a near disaster, when Archie was thoroughly scolded for having unwittingly exposed a trick being performed by the great David Devant by letting a spotlight fall on what was supposed to be a concealed mirror, did not check his wild and growing enthusiasm for the theatre world.

It was enormous fun being even a dogsbody in a busy theatre, with pantomime and vaudeville at its height, but soon Archie craved more. One evening, listening to the talk backstage, he heard someone mention the name Bob Pender and his troupe of young performers. Pender, it seemed, was looking for new lads, his regular troupe being seriously depleted by the war. Archie consulted no one. He hurried home and wrote off at once to Mr Pender saying that he was fourteen (the school-leaving age) and writing in his father's name. By return of post came a letter bidding the boy to come to Norwich, where the Penders were on tour, for an interview.

Very early one morning, saying nothing to his father, Archie packed a bag and caught the milk train from Bristol station. Pender was waiting for him. Archie took instantly to this sturdy, reliable, likeable man, who had been a famous Drury Lane clown. If Pender was suspicious about Archie's age, he was also impressed by the boy's height and build and his obvious eagerness. That same day he gave him a contract as an apprentice, for which he was to receive his keep as well as ten shillings a week pay. By nightfall, Archie was tucked up in bed in the same lodgings as Mr and Mrs Pender and the youngest members of the company. Next morning, he started learning how to become an acrobat.

It took Elias ten days to track down his son. When summons came from the doorkeeper of the theatre in Ipswich where the Pender troupe was playing that a man calling himself his father was waiting for him at the door, Archie sensed that he was doomed. He was at least partially right. Elias was not really angry, but he insisted that the boy return instantly to school. However, he and Pender developed an instant liking for each other, based perhaps on the fact that both were ardent Freemasons. Elias promised to let Archie return to the troupe as soon as he had completed his schooling.

That day came sooner than anyone had anticipated. Archie returned to his companions in a cocky mood, something of a hero. His heroics were not calculated to please a crusty secondary school headmaster, and, shortly after Archie turned fourteen, he found himself expelled from the school for having committed just one misdemeanour too many.

Archie's future now looked, for the time being at least, settled. With his father's permission he rejoined Pender and his boys and started out life as a dancer, tumbler, acrobat, and stilt walker (no easy feat for a boy with a terror of heights) in the vaudeville theatre then at the peak of its popularity, touring from town to town and living out of a suitcase. Archie, a fastidious boy, with an almost obsessive need for cleanliness, did not always find it easy to keep as spotless as he would have liked.

Pender's troupe prospered, and so did Archie. And so no one was particularly surprised when, in the early summer of 1920, Bob Pender announced that he was taking a company of eight boys with him to America, to New York's Globe Theater, and that Archibald Leach was to be one of them.

The troupe, eight ecstatically excited young boys under the watchful eyes of Mr and Mrs Pender, set sail from Southampton docks on the RMS *Olympic*, sistership to the *Titanic* and the world's largest ship, on a bright summer's day in July. Ten years were to pass before Archie caught sight once more of the British coastline. If he had any doubts about the wisdom of what he was doing, or any feelings of sadness about leaving his father, he didn't show them.

On board he had his first experience of stardom. The form it took was an extraordinarily apposite foretaste of what the future held for him. Douglas Fairbanks Senior and Mary Pickford, then at the pinnacle of their world popularity, had chosen the *Olympic* on which to return home from their European honeymoon. Archie watched amazed as the couple were mobbed by autograph hunters and photographers, and he marvelled at their good humour in the face of such constant scrutiny. He had long felt for Douglas Fairbanks an admiration verging on hero worship: his particular combination of athleticism and perfect gentlemanly polish seemed to personify all the young man most aspired to.

One day he found himself standing next to the star as he was playing shuffleboard; shyly, he tried to express something of what he later called 'my adulation'. The encounter left a deep impression on him, so deep in fact that years afterwards he would explain to friends that, 'I've doggedly striven to keep tanned ever since, only because of a desire to emulate his healthful appearance.'

New York in 1920 was the capital, the heart of the world's blossoming entertainment business. The advent of the movies had given a new lease of life to vaudeville and immense palaces of entertainment were springing up all over the city to present combined programmes of film and variety acts. By the time Archie reached New York, electric signs spelling out 'Paramount' and 'Fox' dominated every street, with exhibitors vying with one another for audiences by providing more marble, more arcades of mirrors, more gimmicky acts, and more architecturally outrageous and fascinating theatres. In the Rivoli, which had been open just three years, ushers wore scarlet tunics piped in gold across the front with more gold and tassels, and carried swagger sticks with mother-of-pearl tips that lit up in the dark.

The RMS *Olympic* docked off Manhattan Island on a very hot early morning. On reaching the Globe Theater the Penders learned that the arrangements for their stay in New York had in fact been altered while they were at sea and that they were now booked to appear at the Hippodrome instead. The switch was a great honour, but it was also daunting: the Hippodrome, standing on Sixth Avenue, was not merely the largest theatre in New York, but commonly believed to be the largest in the world, playing to over 10,000 people a week and presenting acts from all over the world on a revolving stage a city block wide and half a block deep. The Pender boys found themselves billed alongside Marceline the clown, Joe Jackson the tramp cyclist, a herd of performing elephants, and a corps of girl swimmers executing incredible stunts in a tank containing nearly a million gallons of water. Among the glamour and the bustle, more military manoeuvre than stage performance — counting performers and non-performers, there were 1,800 people involved backstage with every show — the eight British teenagers felt young and inexperienced.

Outside theatre hours the Penders settled their troupe in a nearby rented flat, built rather like a train compartment with doors opening off each other down a long corridor. A strict regime was soon instigated whereby each boy had to fulfil his rota of duties. Archie's scouting had made him an exellent stew chef. The flat was just off Times Square and, to a group of provincial English boys, extremely noisy. Streetcars and heavily laden trucks and vans rumbled up and down Eighth Avenue all night, police sirens wailed, and from Ninth Avenue, a block away, could be heard the famous elevated train, the El, as it hurtled past overhead on its steel girders.

The troupe may have been young, but they were by now seasoned professionals and the American audiences loved them. When the Hippodrome booking came to an end, their act was picked up by the prestigious Keith vaudeville circuit and the Penders immediately embarked on a tour of Boston, Washington, Chicago, Philadelphia, Cleveland, Kansas City, Salt Lake City, Seattle, and Los Angeles. Everywhere the boys were praised and fêted. In Atlantic City they were introduced to Jack Dempsey, heavyweight boxing champion of the world. In Washington they met congressmen and presidential aides.

When it was all over and it was time to go home, Archie had other plans. He had been dazzled by the America he had seen, and more than that he believed that he had a future there. Somewhat to his surprise Bob Pender gave him his blessing, and backed it up with the generous gift of enough money to cover his passage home, to keep in reserve for the day that he should need it. The Pender troupe then sailed away.

The summer of 1922 was not a happy one for Archie. It was true that he had four years of solid performing behind him, but he had never actually been in a play, or spoken a single word of dialogue on stage. What was more, without the troupe, he didn't have much to sell, for he had no specific act of his own. As the summer wore on, and his fare home was eaten into, while booking agent after booking agent warned him that there wasn't much work around, Archie grew decidedly anxious.

He must, however, have been a charmer. There was something about this stylish eighteen-year-old, with his English accent and his consistently neat turnout that seemed to bewitch all who came in touch with him. Before the summer was out, Archie had been taken up by smart New Yorkers who invited him to their dinner parties. One evening he was even detailed to act as escort to the famed soprano Lucrezia Bori.

But none of this brought in cash and Archie was soon obliged to take a job as a stilt walker on Coney Island, advertising Tilyou's Steeplechase Park to the tourists who flocked to the amusement arcades. It was hardly stardom, but it paid well – $5 a day Monday to Friday, $10 for Saturdays and Sundays – and Archie was never a boy to indulge in a sense of false pride. Fearing hard times ahead, he saved and hoarded.

By September's Labour Day, when the stilt-walking job ended, he had the good fortune to be befriended by a young man called Orry-Kelly who was himself struggling to find work – and who would eventually become an Oscar-winning costume designer – and was now busy hand painting men's ties. He invited Archie to sell them for him, on a commission, and before long the young vaudeville artist was peddling ties along Sixth Avenue and in Greenwich Village.

Archie never forgot the theatre. Even as he was hawking his wares, he was deep in plans to put together a company of acts like his own, and rehearsing and discussing with other young out-of-work performers. When their show was ready, they had little difficulty selling themselves on a second-rank circuit tour. The new troupe set out: first to the small towns of the East Coast, then up to Canada and back across the country from California to New York.

In 1924, having saved some money, the group disbanded. The different acts went their different ways and Archie went back to New York to embark on a fresh search for work. He became a juggler, a dancer, a unicycle rider, a comedian, and an illusionist. He even worked as the audience plant for a mind-reading act. He played in theatres and in clubs, in church halls, at Moose clubs, at anniversaries, and Bar Mitzvahs. He didn't become rich. But he became very professional and very accomplished indeed.

And then one day a friend introduced him to Reggie Hammerstein, who took him to see his uncle Arthur Hammerstein, then about to begin rehearsals for an operetta called *Golden Dawn*. Archie was by now twenty-three, tall, extremely good looking, and could sing. He was offered the part of an Australian prisoner of war, a role that carried with it the secondary love interest. It was the moment of reckoning. Could this vaudeville pro actually speak? Archie had been on the boards for ten years and there was almost nothing he couldn't do once he put his mind to it. He made extremely sure that speech was no exception.

Golden Dawn, which opened on Broadway in the autumn of 1927 (just as the first talkie, *The Jazz Singer*, was released on an unsuspecting world), was not a hit. But by the time it closed, after 184 performances, Arthur Hammerstein had taken a liking to his young English recruit and offered him the lead in a forthcoming musical to be called *Polly*. The offer was premature: Archie didn't yet have the experience for the full range of musical comedy and critics panned his performance at the trial runs in Wilmington, Delaware.

In the American show business world of the 1920s artists usually had long-term contracts with theatrical entrepreneurs, who handled their bookings, controlled what parts they played, and guaranteed them a regular salary. The deal provided security, but when a performer was popular it could be extremely cramping. Not long after *Polly* closed, Marilyn Miller asked for Archie as the replacement for her leading man, Jack Donahue, in the Ziegfeld hit *Rosalie*. The part might have made Archie. The trouble was that Hammerstein and Ziegfeld hated one another passionately and Hammerstein had no intention of releasing a promising young star to his bitter enemy. Instead, he handed over the boy to the Shuberts for three full years of operetta. Archie was to remember the transaction.

As it was, he could have done worse. The Shuberts were unique in the history of American show business for the range and quantity

31

of their enterprises. They owned theatres in New York and many others in the major American cities; they held the rights to dozens of musicals, dramas, and operettas, and they controlled the lives of hundreds of rising stars. And they had taken a fancy to Archie. Less than a week after they had taken over his contract, Archie found himself cast in a new musical called *Boom-Boom*.

The Shuberts began by offering him the enormous sum of $450 a week. But Archie, remembering Hammerstein, had other ideas. He asked to be let off the clause binding him to the company whether he was working or not and to be given a simple run-of-the-show contract. He offered to take less money. The Shuberts, astonished at such courage and independence, agreed, and gave him the full $450 a week just the same.

Boom-Boom was a smash hit. Both Jeanette MacDonald, the female lead, and Archie were invited by Paramount to come and be tested at their Astoria studio. Afterwards they agreed that their first appearance before cameras had been a 'torture test' and that neither had a chance of a future in the film world. They were at least half wrong. Jeanette MacDonald was summoned to Hollywood to sing with Nelson Eddy. As for Archie, he was told: 'You're bow-legged and your neck is too thick.'

And so Archie stayed in New York with the Shuberts, playing in operettas, picking up good reviews, but always just failing to hit the big time. To make up for it, he took to enjoying New York society and the smart set, frequenting the Algonquin Hotel where the theatre people and the writers met and talked about life. When he had nothing else to do, he hung around Rudley's Restaurant on Broadway with all the other young actors looking for parts. It was a pleasant existence, and by any standard a comfortable one – for by now Archie was commanding between $300–$450 a week. But there was something missing.

A couple of years earlier Archie had put some of his first serious earnings into a Packard, a great gleaming touring car. Now, as the last of his Broadway appearances, as a young man called Cary Lockwood in the play *Nikki* by John Monk Sanders, starring his wife Fay Wray, came to an end, he decided that he was entitled to a holiday. He sublet his small apartment, packed his belongings into the boot of the Packard, and set off west – for Hollywood.

3

On Becoming
Cary Grant

In the late autumn of 1931, as Archie Leach drove his Packard west, America was at the worst of the Depression. In every town through which he drove the streets were lined with queues of the hungry and the unemployed hoping for food from the soup kitchens. Everywhere, there was dereliction, poverty, despair.

But as he entered California the air lightened, the colours grew brighter, and the smells stronger. In Hollywood life seemed much as it had on previous visits, with the clear, almost Mediterranean blue of the sky and the palm trees lining the broad boulevards. But there was a difference: the economic collapse that had spelt such misery for so many millions of people had spelt a boom for the movie business. Now, as never before, audiences craved oblivion in comedies and fantasies and splendour. They found it in the popular new talkies and in the great musicals of the 1930s, and they found it, too, in the cinemas themselves, vast rococo and Moorish palaces of entertainment, with their fountains and waterfalls, their painted peacocks and doves, their mirrors and arcades and galleries, all designed to provide, for a few hours at least, an illusion of prosperity.

Vaudeville could have no place in all this excessive splendour, and the Los Angeles that Archie entered was fast shedding, like every other city in America, its music halls, selling them off to the film studios who were desperate to get control of as many guaranteed outlets as they could for the hundreds of films now pouring so successfully off their production lines.

It might have fared badly for Archie had he not, before leaving Broadway, been given the address of a movie contact in Hollywood who took to him and soon introduced him to the head of Paramount Studios, B.P. Schulberg. Over dinner Schulberg invited Archie to make a screen test, and after seeing it offered him a contract at $450 a week, stipulating only that a better name than Archibald Leach be found for his new movie actor. Archie went off to consult his New York theatre friend, Fay Wray, and between them they came up with the idea of using Cary Lockwood, the name of the character he had played in *Nikki*.

Paramount didn't like Lockwood. It was too long and, what was more, there was already a film actor called Harold Lockwood – that could only lead to confusion. Someone got out a list of names – the fashion of the day was for the shorter, two- or three-syllable names like Tracy, Cagney, or Cooper – and the pin stopped on Grant. A couple of days later, on 7 December 1931, a Bristol music-hall juvenile called Archibald Leach turned into a Hollywood film star by the name of Cary Grant.

It was a while, however, before Grant – the name Leach was shed for evermore – reached real stardom. What he did, for that first year at least, was work: fifty-two straight weeks in 1932, with never more than two days running off at any one time, and seven films to his credit, some good parts, some bad, but on the go all the time, sometimes acting in two films at the same time. 'No great shakes as an actor,' a critic once wrote, 'but he has a certain niftiness.'

The transformation to box office idol came not long after the end of his first year in Hollywood. It was one of those combinations of chance, talent, and charm that seem to mark so much of Grant's career. The story, so well known as to sound almost apocryphal, is that Grant was returning to the set of *Madame Butterfly* (a film rendering of the Puccini opera) after lunch in the studio canteen, still decked out in his white naval uniform and glamorously tanned by the Californian sun, when Mae West happened to be climbing out of her car. Mae West was Paramount's prize star and she was currently on the look out for a male lead for a new film, to be called *She Done Him Wrong*. 'If he can talk,' she said to the Paramount vice-president hovering at her side, and pointing in the direction of the vanishing naval uniform, 'I'll take him.'

She Done Him Wrong was an immense box office success. It put Grant, overnight, up among the stars, with the same billing as Carole Lombard and Frederic March. Paramount, cashing in on the enormous profits of the partnership between Grant and Mae West, rushed out a follow-up, *I'm No Angel*, providing Grant with the chance to repeat his new-found genius for flatly delivered, wry, *double entendre* comedy. Grant never forgot his debt to Mae West. 'I learned everything from her,' he was to say years later, when anyone brought up the early days. 'Well, not everything, but almost everything. She knows so much. Her instinct is so true, her timing so perfect, her grasp of the situation so right.'

Now began a period of remarkable glamour and success for the twenty-nine-year-old Englishman: six movies in 1933, four in 1934. He complemented them by getting married, after a short, much commented-on romance, to Virginia Cherrill, the wan and touching star of Charlie Chaplin's silent *City Lights* (who had already had two husbands, Irving Adler and William Rhinelander Stewart). The ceremony took place in London, at Caxton Hall registry office, since both bride and groom were English; they were mobbed by fans and harassed by reporters. The barrage of publicity kept up when they returned to Hollywood and Grant reported the disappearance of his much-loved Sealyham terrier, only to be inundated by hourly and fictitious reports of the dog's sighting.

It was not an auspicious way to begin a marriage and matters did not improve. Grant was constantly busy, constantly working; Virginia was increasingly lonely. When they separated, after a bare seven months of marriage, the incident was marked by drama; Grant was discovered by a servant unconscious at two-thirty in the morning, a bottle of pills by the bed. Later he explained that he had merely been blind drunk. Whatever had happened, the press loved it.

Grant didn't take long to recover. He was barely thirty, superbly good looking, and as greatly in demand by the studios as by women. Characteristically, he concentrated on work, though he was somewhat galled to find that he tended to be put in films Gary Cooper was too busy to take on, or, worse, imitations of Cooper successes. Still, he was making an impact with leading ladies – Katharine Hepburn, Joan Bennett – which was to prove one of the most attractive hallmarks of his particular kind of performance.

He was also busy concentrating on himself. After the divorce he moved into a house in Santa Monica with a friend called Randolph Scott and began to emulate his first flesh-and-blood hero, Douglas Fairbanks Senior, whose air of healthy vigour he had so admired on board the RMS *Olympic* fifteen years earlier. He became a sun addict. Whenever there was a pause during daylight hours he would stretch out and bake in the hot Californian glare, either at home by his pool or on the studio lot in between takes. He stopped wearing make-up for his parts, relying instead on skin now dyed a permanent tanned hue, and on his natural healthiness.

In February 1937 Grant's contract with Paramount came to an end. The studio moguls confidently prepared to draw up another. But Grant, who had taken a long, close look at the industry, and was in any case far from happy with the system whereby stars were tied up for years at a time to a single studio, with little real power over their own destinies, now made a move reminiscent of the one he had made so long before on Broadway. He refused to sign another exclusive contract – with Paramount or anyone else. With an already finely tuned sense of business acumen and canny foresightedness, he had quite simply decided that he would be better off on his own. That year, he became Hollywood's first freelance star.

As with his later business enterprises, he had acted with considerable shrewdness. He had been earning $5,000 a week at Paramount: he was soon to be bringing in $300,000 for every major picture he turned out, and there was no shortage of suitors for his services. Grant's release from Paramount marked the start of a patch of unparalleled screen success, with romantic comedies and melodramas following one upon the last, and perfectly pitched partnerships with Irene Dunne and Katharine Hepburn, in *Holiday, My Favourite Wife, The Philadelphia Story.* Sidney Grauman, of Grauman's Chinese Theater, with its pagodas and festooned dragons, conferred on him Hollywood's finest accolade – his footprint in cement in the cinema forecourt, to join those of Douglas Fairbanks and Gary Cooper, in a ceremony full of laughter and publicity. Afterwards he was interviewed by Louella Parsons, doyen of Hollywood's press corps.

Never had Grant been more part of the Hollywood movie community. In the early spring of 1942 he joined the biggest screen names – Bing Crosby, Bob Hope, Claudette Colbert, James Cagney, Laurel and Hardy – on a three-week whistle-stop tour of America, raising money for the war effort. Every actor had his own luxurious compartment on the train, which was equipped with barbers and hairdressers, chaperones to keep the moral tone high, and a doctor to furnish sleeping pills for the nights and benzedrine for the mornings. It was all very symbolic of Hollywood's royal status. When the caravan came into a town in the morning, the stars would be conveyed to hotels to rest. In the afternoon they turned out to parade through the streets, then went on to give a three-hour extravaganza, after which they would descend into the audience and ask for money for the war effort.

Never had Grant been working better as an actor and, as he said himself, never had he learned so much. *Sylvia Scarlett*, released in 1936, brought him directly in contact with a movie maker of real worth: George Cukor. In *Sylvia Scarlett*, Grant played a cockney petty crook, a tricky, brash con-man with appallingly loud suits. He started out, Cukor said later, 'rather wooden'. By the end of the shooting, he had 'suddenly burst into bloom'. Of the experience, Grant himself said: 'I learned comedy timing from George; the whole part gave me a new lease of life as a comedian.' It was for Cukor that Grant went on to make *Holiday* and *The Philadelphia Story*.

These were also the years that produced Grant's vastly successful *Arsenic and Old Lace*, directed by Frank Capra, and the start of his rich association with Alfred Hitchcock, in *Suspicion*, to be

39

followed in time by *Notorious*, which partnered Grant for the first time with Ingrid Bergman and produced the longest kiss in the history of guilt-ridden, Hayes-code-obsessed Hollywood. (Since they had to do take after take to get the kiss absolutely right, they took to whispering what looked like sweet nothings in each other's ears as they embraced, but which were in fact mostly prosaic remarks about whose turn it was to do the washing up.) Grant was to say that he and Hitchcock got on so well together from the start because of their shared memory for Liquorice-All-Sorts. Whatever the reason, Hitchcock had an immense amount of respect for Grant, and would accept suggestions for direction that he would not have taken easily from many others.

Into Grant's performances, both on stage and off, was entering a spirit of lively self-mockery that made him, sometimes, draw reality into the fantasy world of the screen, as a kind of comic spoof on his own life. He used his real name (long a joke to himself and to the public, particularly after he named his Sealyham dog Archibald and the dog escaped) both in *Gunga Din*, when Grant, as a soldier, receives an invitation to a regimental ball and reads out 'Archibald Leach' enunciating every syllable with disbelief at its absurdity, and in *His Girl Friday*, when, as editor of a newspaper, he is threatened with prison by the sheriff and snaps: 'The last man to say that to me was Archie Leach, just a week before he cut his throat.'

Outside the studios, Grant's life was changing. He was making new friends, people like Howard Hughes who he got to know when Hughes bought RKO Studios and flew him off to Mexico on jaunts in his converted bomber (and who he was later to describe, appreciatively, as someone who did not interfere) or Countess Dorothy di Frasso, the society hostess who lived on a $1 million trust fund left by her father and who held court on both sides of the Atlantic and thought it amusing to invite gangsters (she called them 'characters') to her parties. It was in fact through the countess that Grant met Barbara Hutton, daughter of F.W. Woolworth, by then twice divorced, and about whom the newspapers kept up a constant barrage of speculation as to whether she was the first or second richest girl in the world. (The other contender for the title was Doris Duke, the tobacco heiress.) For Grant, this was a time of glittering and incessant parties, sophisticated and affluent new friends, and all the paraphernalia of Californian high society.

In July 1942, still a top box office star, but somewhat less suited to the movies coming his way in wartime Hollywood, Grant officially became an American citizen and legally changed his name from Leach to Grant. Shortly afterwards, he went off on a brief holiday to Lake Arrowhead to see his agent Frank Vincent and there, in total secrecy, having been bruised by the press before, he married Barbara Hutton, under an oak tree in the garden. This time the gossip columnists did not let him off lightly.

Stories suggesting that he had become an American citizen only in order to escape war service for his own country (he did in fact apply to join the Army Air Corps but was rejected) or barely veiled accounts of his activities as a 'social climber' began to appear regularly in the movie gossip columns. Someone nicknamed them 'Cash' and 'Carry'. (It was not until many years later that it became known that Grant had insisted on signing a statement relinquishing any claim to Barbara Hutton's fortune in the event of a divorce, or that he had donated handsomely to the war effort.) As it was, the slander merely served to alienate a man already anxious about publicity still further from collaboration with newspaper writers, and strengthen an already keen resolve to remain, off screen, a wholly private citizen. It was an experience he was never altogether to recover from.

At first, Grant and Barbara appeared happy. They gave each other handsome presents – Grant wore a Cartier pearl stick pin from her at the wedding – and rented Douglas Fairbanks Junior's house on Pacific Palisades. They took on eleven servants. Lance, Barbara's six-year-old son by a Danish count called Haugwitz von Reventlow, came to live with them and Grant, long eager to have children of his own and saddened by the brevity of his first marriage, took greatly to the small boy.

It was a time of family life and family commitments. After twenty years of belief that his mother had somehow vanished, Grant

41

learned that she was in fact alive, healthy but in a mental institution. When his father died (of 'extreme toxicity', having been living with another woman and having had a child by her) Grant arranged, together with her cousins and relations, to move her to a house of her own in Bristol – no one felt that she could be uprooted and moved to a world as different as that of California – where they could keep an eye on her, and which he could visit whenever he could get away from Hollywood. Amazingly, after twenty years imprisoned in a mental hospital, Elsie Leach was able to cope with normal life. For Grant, however, the discovery of a lost mother, and the realization that she had spent so long in acute misery, was a confusing and traumatic experience.

Soon, however, there were problems with his new marriage. Grant, who worked, as he always had, extremely hard, leaving for the studio not long after dawn and returning towards six, liked to spend his evenings in tranquillity at home, memorizing his lines for the next day's shooting. Barbara, who was bored in Hollywood and beginning to yearn for her Monte Carlo and Venetian friends, started to complain that Grant was not the man she thought she was marrying, the star of *The Philadelphia Story*, 'fun, laughing, and naughty all the time'. On the contrary, he was serious and he craved order and routine. She took to having dinner parties; Grant took to coming home from the studio and taking his dinner to bed.

For a while, they hung on. Barbara was providing Grant with something that he had never really had before, a taste of style, as well as an education in music and art. She gave him a Boudin and an Utrillo, and two Tiepolo drawings that he kept by him for many years after their separation. In return he gave, or tried to give, a sense of stability. In the end, however, there was simply too much that was wrong: too many differences of opinion, too great a dislike of each other's friends, too marked a conflict of behaviour. In August 1945 the Grants were divorced. 'I shall never remarry again,' Barbara told reporters in New York before taking off for Europe with Lance, where she bought a twenty-room palace in the Casbah in Tangier.

As for Grant, he left the Douglas Fairbanks mansion with all the servants who had oppressed him, and at last bought a small house of his own in the valleys above Beverly Hills. It was more bungalow than mansion, but with spectacular views across the city, perched high out above a canyon, with a steep drop on all sides around, and barely another house in sight. He had ambitious architectural plans for his new house, but postponed all alterations by throwing himself energetically into *Night and Day* for Warners, a film based on the life of Cole Porter. Once again work, solid, regular, and conducted wholly professionally, provided him with a steadying framework. He was about due for a run of good films. After *Night and Day* Alfred Hitchcock came up with one, *Notorious*, giving him the opportunity of acting with Ingrid Bergman, one of the happiest partnerships of his career.

Off screen, his life was more erratic. Two brief and unhappy marriages had made him wary of commitments, and he was reluctant in any case to feed the Hollywood gossip columnists with more stories than he could help. (Avoiding publicity altogether was impossible. When there was nothing to say, the columnists invented something. But Grant did his best.)

Then a more serious figure entered his life. Late in 1947, as he sailed back to the States on board the *Queen Mary* after a visit to his mother in Bristol, he was introduced by Merle Oberon to an American actress called Betsy Drake, who was returning home from a successful London run of *Deep Are the Roots*. She was the granddaughter of the man who had founded the famous Drake Hotel in Chicago. Betsy Drake was twenty-four, slight, fair-haired and blue-eyed, a young woman of considerable intelligence and humour. By the time the ship docked, they were friends.

A few weeks later Betsy followed Grant back to California, where he introduced her to David Selznick and Howard Hughes and before long secured for her a leading role opposite himself in *Every Girl Should be Married*. On Christmas Day 1949, in Phoenix, Arizona, he married her. Howard Hughes, Grant's best man, had flown the couple to his ranch in his private plane, and later arranged for a brief honeymoon on board his yacht which, Grant told Bill Weaver many years later, he had specially positioned at such an angle that all night the beams from the full moon shone directly through the porthole of their stateroom. It was romance all right, Hollywood style.

This time, Grant looked set for happiness. He gave his new wife a diamond clasp and a miniature poodle, installed her in his house, which he had still not touched, and returned to work. The arrangement suited Betsy. She didn't like glamour and didn't care much about décor, and soon filled the house, not with *bijou* knick-knacks or decorator's treasures, but with the paraphernalia of her own hobbies – photographic equipment and typewriters. (Grant complained about the mess.) She gave up acting, saying that she hated it. Extremely rich – Grant's fortune was now put at about between $10 and $15 million, some $1 billion by today's equivalent – they chose to live extremely simply, taking more pleasure in their own company and very little indeed in social Hollywood which buzzed around them. In due course, they bought themselves a second house, in Palm Springs, where they went when Grant could get time off from the studios. (They also bought themselves two Rolls-Royces, one for California and one for London.)

Betsy's naturally inquisitive and enquiring mind, as well as the fact that she had a great deal of time and not much to do in it, attracted her early on towards the occult and the powers of hypnotism. Grant had long been a chain smoker. Betsy maintained that she could cure him. After one session, she apparently did so, for Grant declared that a curtain had come down on him and that smoking ceased to have any appeal for him. He never smoked again. 'I'm learning to relax,' he told friends. 'If you decide that you are going to be youthful and fit for the rest of your life, you will be. It's as simple as that.'

Grant was, at last, happy. Betsy was the perfect companion for him, and they had a great deal of fun together. But he had always been a restless, somewhat uneasy figure, quick to find fault with himself, acutely indecisive and easily fretful, and none of this changed with marriage, however loving his partner. It was Betsy who now encouraged him to experiment with a new drug, LSD, that had just appeared on the market, and which was reputed to have a marvellous capacity for breaking down the voluntary blocks on memory, thus releasing the emotions and experiences of the past. Grant, long brooding on the turmoils of his own childhood, and curious to understand what effects the loss of his mother and his parents' unhappiness might have had on him, began to attend LSD sessions under a Dr Mortimer Hartman, who administered the drug and watched over the hallucinogenic reactions of his patients in a setting of soft lights and meaningful music. Usually Grant went alone; occasionally he was part of a group of friends, among them Aldous Huxley, all seeking further enlightenment about the traumas of the human mind.

The effect of LSD on Grant was startling. For the first time he not only tolerated reporters' questions but actively sought out interviews in which he proclaimed: 'I have just been born again.' The usual self-deprecating manner, so charming on screen and so infuriating to gossip columnists, was replaced by a mood of intense self-revelation. He talked freely about his marriages, his insecurities, even his mother who, now that he could once again bear to think about her without pain, resumed an important role in his life. He told a group of students at UCLA: 'I was a self-centred boor – a masochist who only thought I was happy. Then I woke up and said: "There must be something wrong with me." I grew up . . . I learned to accept the responsibility for my own actions and to blame myself and no one else for the circumstances of my own creating. I learned that no one else was keeping me unhappy but me; that I could whip myself better than any other guy in the joint.' (When Mae West heard of Grant's experiments with LSD she commented wryly: 'What is Cary fooling with that stuff for? Why doesn't he come up and see me sometime? I'll straighten him out.')

The new-found steadfastness of character and serenity of spirit was not to last. In the mid-1950s, Stanley Kramer invited Grant to take one of the leading roles in *The Pride and the Passion* which he was about to start shooting in Spain. Frank Sinatra was to be the other male lead, and Kramer was hoping to get Ava Gardner for the female star. In the end, the part fell to the young and then virtually unknown Sophia Loren.

In her own autobiography, written many years later, she recalled her first meeting with Grant. 'How do you do, Miss Lolloloren, or is it Lorenigida? Ah, you Italian actresses, I can never get your names straight.' He exuded charm, and he was even more handsome and debonair than he appeared on screen.

The sense of approval and attraction was clearly mutual and before long Sophia Loren and Grant, thrown cosily together for the best part of six months in a remote part of Spain, spending their days on the set and their evenings alone in small country restaurants, grew deeply entangled. For a while, as Sophia Loren was to explain later, Grant even talked to her about marriage, and she was seriously tempted to break off her relationship with Carlo Ponti. But she decided not to. What Grant really thought about it all he kept, characteristically, to himself.

Sometime towards the end of filming, Betsy came out to Spain to pay a visit to her husband. A couple of weeks later she left to board the *Andrea Doria* at Gibraltar for the voyage home. In the middle of the night, when the boat stood not far out from the coast of Nantucket, it collided with a Swedish liner called the *Stockholm*. The *Stockholm* managed to stay afloat, but the *Andrea Doria*, taking fifty-six people with her, sank to the bottom of the sea.

Betsy was not one of them (though all her possessions, including a collection of shirts specially made for Grant that she was taking home for him, were lost) and she managed to get a cable sent to Grant from the wireless of the ship that picked up the survivors. 'I'm safe,' it said, 'thank God. Don't worry. Love Betsy.' It was the first that Grant had heard of the accident.

The collision probably postponed what was beginning to friends to look like a permanent rupture between the two of them. But at last, in October 1958 (having been married nearly ten years – something of a record for Grant, and more than twice his previous marriages put together), they agreed to separate. 'We had to part,' explained Grant later, 'that was inevitable, there was something wrong and we knew it.'

Betsy, who told reporters that she was still in love with him, added that he 'appeared to be bored with me. I became lonely, unhappy, miserable ... He showed no interest in any of my friends.' Grant, as usual, said nothing, beyond lamenting the end of the marriage.

The effects of the LSD, conferring on him as it had an illusion of greater self-understanding and the ability to commit himself properly to one woman, had been short lived. Grant retreated back up to his mountain home, and filled his work hours with a film that allowed him to be even more himself than usual – the Cary Grant of the screen, wry, charming, self-deprecating, stylish. It was Alfred Hitchcock's *North by Northwest*. The private Grant, for a while at least, vanished from sight. The public version, as desirable, good looking and plausible as ever, took the dominant role once again.

4

Hard Times in Benedict Canyon

These were not happy years for Grant. He was on his own, nearing sixty, with three marriages behind him, no children, and no obvious sense of newness or future in his films. The screen character Grant had created, with the beautiful tailored clothes, the nonchalance, the polish, and the exquisite sense of timing, had now long been perfected. But where was it to go? True, Grant had aged better than any man in Hollywood: he was really better looking than when he had first arrived in California, more solid, more steady, but every bit as glamorous. If anything, the screen partnerships – most recently Ingrid Bergman and Audrey Hepburn – were more sexy than his earlier relationships with leading ladies.

Yet, as he made clear in a serialized autobiography printed around this time in the *Ladies' Home Journal*, the assurance did not go deep. There is something wistful in the tone of this curiously self-revealing portrait. 'I am not proud of my marriage career,' he writes. 'It was not the fault of Hollywood, but my own inadequacies. Of my own inconstancy. My mistrust of constancy . . . I feel fine. Alone. But fine. My mother is quite elderly. My wives have divorced me, and I await a woman with the best qualities of each. I will endow her with those qualities because they will be in my own point of view.' For all the optimism, there is something a little valedictory in the speech, the words of a man surveying the past with nostalgia.

In point of fact, Grant did not have long to wait for a new companion. In 1961, he was looking around the movie world for a young girl to take a part in a film he was considering when he happened to catch sight of a photograph in the *Hollywood Reporter*. It was of Diane Frieson, and she was advertising a television series called *The Aquanauts*. He called her agent and fixed an appointment for an interview.

Diane turned out to be too old for the part – she confessed to nineteen and was in fact twenty-two – but she and Grant got on well and soon started going out together around Los Angeles, to the delight of the columnists, who soon unearthed her past as a graduate of UCLA now trying to make her way in bit parts and television serials in Hollywood.

Grant's increasingly public friendship with Dyan Cannon – she had by now been fetchingly renamed 'Dyan' by an Italian newspaper reporter who got the spelling of her name wrong, and she had picked up the 'Cannon', like all other stars, at the studios – did a lot for the aspiring actress. Cheesecake appearances, in bikini or revealing dress, were soon replaced by more serious roles, as she began to absorb something of Grant's seriousness and repute. But, as friends were quick to spot, there was more to their relationship than the courting of a useful ageing star by an ambitious up-and-coming starlet. Dyan admired Grant and was learning a lot from him – how to dress, how to appear more natural – and she wasn't overawed by him. They laughed together. As for Grant, coach, tutor, and companion, he began emerging from behind the public screen image and once again stopped being so prickly when the couple were deluged by Hollywood press reporters when they attended a movie première or went off to swim on Malibu Beach.

On Thursday, 22 July 1965, a Hollywood gossip writer included a short item in her nationally syndicated column: 'Someone better warn Dyan Cannon,' it said, 'that Cary Grant may not find time to marry her!' The columnist was wrong. That same day, as millions were reading the words coast to coast across America, Dyan and Grant were in the process of getting married in Las Vegas. So secret was the event – this time Grant was absolutely determined not to spoil the occasion – that it was not made public until 1

August, eleven days later, and by then the couple had taken flight to England and were ensconced in the Royal Hotel in Bristol, on a visit to Grant's eighty-seven-year-old mother. Though besieged by the world's press corps when the news got out, they managed to escape relatively unharmed by harassment, helped by hotel managers and a smooth chauffeur, and on returning to Hollywood settled down to Grant's invariable domestic routine: hard work, few social engagements, and as much privacy as they could engineer. There was no more talk of Dyan's future career as an actress.

That autumn, Grant was to play in a new film, *Walk, Don't Run*, to be shot largely in Japan. Somewhat to Hollywood's surprise, he left for Tokyo on his own, while Dyan was widely reported to be 'resting' and 'out of town'.

The reticence, for once in Grant's marital life, marked not ominous signs of friction, but wonderful news. There was nothing at all wrong with the couple's relationship. On the contrary, something had happened that was to transform Grant's life drastically and for ever: Dyan was pregnant. On 14 October Associated Press released a bald statement: 'Cary Grant,' said the bulletin, as it flashed out over the world wires, 'is expecting his first child next May, when he will be sixty-two.' It was the event he had been waiting for all his life.

Dyan's pregnancy was, at first at least, an easy one, but Grant, ever a worrier, fretted away about the coming baby's well-being. On this occasion his doubts and fears might have proved justified. On 26 February, some ten weeks early, Dyan went into labour. That night, after Grant had spent an interminable day in the father's room of the hospital, she was delivered of a four-pound eight-ounce girl. The baby was put in an incubator, but she was fit and strong. 'I'm the world's worst worrier,' Grant told journalists. 'Dyan had the baby and I did the worrying.'

The anxiety for the child's welfare – she had by now been named Jennifer – persisted long after she was allowed home, and it was not until the early summer, shortly before the Grants were due to sail for Europe to show Elsie her granddaughter, that photographers were finally permitted to come to the house and view the baby. Pictures of the occasion, Dyan clasping Jennifer in her arms, Grant beaming over her shoulder, appeared in every newspaper in the world.

Earlier that summer Grant had decided that he needed a new secretary. His resident helper, Dorothy, had been with him for seven years, but for most of these Grant had been struggling and failing to ease her out of his life. She was middle-aged, affectionate, and possessive. What was more, he had come to the conclusion that he needed a man rather than a woman to work for him, someone with high secretarial qualifications and proven trustworthiness, but who could also carry suitcases, stave off importunate reporters, and drive the Rolls.

That same spring, Bill Weaver, a twenty-five-year-old bachelor from Kansas, had come to Hollywood in search of a new life. He was a somewhat nervous young man, but he possessed extremely impressive commercial credentials (top of his school in typing and shorthand) for which he seemed to have a kind of uncanny flair, and a deep love of the theatre. He had never been to college, having spent the years he might have gone helping his mother raise five younger children after his stepfather's death, but somewhere along the line, irregularly and in night school, he had picked up a master's degree in English, while paying his family's way by working for a prime contractor of the Atomic Energy Commission. His mother had recently remarried and Weaver, more interested in acting than in atomic science, had spent the previous six months observing life on Broadway. He had then come west to see if California provided more opportunity. Hearing of Grant's search for a male secretary, he reasoned that this way, at least, he would get a glimpse of the movie world.

Weaver soon discovered that he had made it to the last shortlist. His actual interview with Grant took place in the star's bungalow on the Universal Studio lot, where he was just winding up the filming of *Walk, Don't Run*. The office was rather sumptuous, all brown leather and white curtains, more house than business room, and the cabin was parked, together with those of Universal's élite actors, just inside the entrance to the studio. Grant was kindly, courteous, but somewhat intimidating. He asked Weaver to sit in a squashy, low armchair, into which the young man sank deeply, while he took for himself the tall, imposing wood-and-leather chair behind the desk, from which he peered down on the unfortunate interviewee in a somewhat lofty manner. Weaver noticed that the room beyond contained a brilliant yellow Mexican table, handpainted with flowers, and felt a little like a peon, called to wait upon the master.

Clearly, however, Grant took to him. He seemed to like Weaver's modesty about his background and his achievements, and was impressed by the atomic security clearance he possessed, guarantee of an ability to keep secrets. After their talk, he offered him the job; the money wasn't lavish, but Weaver had no hesitation about accepting.

There was only one snag. Dorothy had not yet been persuaded to leave, and it was some weeks before Weaver was snugly installed at her desk. He soon settled into an enjoyable working routine. He rented a furnished apartment in Hollywood and reported to the bungalow at Universal every morning by nine, having quickly learned that Grant was an early riser and exacted strict punctuality from those he employed. There was still a certain amount of work to be done on *Walk, Don't Run*, now in its closing stages of production, but they were mostly dubbing and administrative chores, which Grant, as co-producer, was eager to supervise. Studio life was busy but fascinating, the days punctuated by the sudden appearance of other film actors on the lot, dropping in for tea or a drink, or social engagements which Weaver would arrange, booking tables at Grant's favourite restaurants like Scandia or the Polo Lounge of the Beverly Hills Hotel, and ensuring that all plans went smoothly, without harassment, particularly from reporters. The bungalow was always full of life and noise, with Stanley Fox, Grant's attorney and a former naval captain, installed at one end in a room full of burgundy-coloured leather furniture, with photographs of Grant hanging on the walls, and Joe Marin, his accountant, alongside.

53

The office-cum-bungalow was an excellent spot from which to view the full flavour of Hollywood movie life. For one thing, it was tucked just inside the immense Universal lot, convenient for passers-by as they arrived or left the studio, yet secluded enough to provide total privacy. Peggy Lee and Cy Colman would suddenly appear at the door one day, and the party would settle down to play the piano and sing songs, and the next day Tony Curtis would bang on the window. For another, it was an attractive place to work, with its enormous sitting room and its mixture of highly modern furniture and Spanish antiques. A designer had clearly been at work – chocolate-coloured leather chairs – but Grant's hand was everywhere: in the spinet piano at which he would sit, tapping out old songs, snatches of jazz, the theme songs from some of his movies; in the white and yellow canvas curtains that covered every window (a real Grant obsession, as Weaver was later to learn); in the handwoven Argentinian rug, with its bright colours and primitive figures that covered the sitting room floor; in the *trompe-l'oeil* painting on every available flat bit of surface so that nothing seemed what it appeared to be, and there were birds and flowers and clouds everywhere; in the wedding pictures of Elsie and Elias Leach in their silver Cartier frames on the desk alongside a framed photograph given to Grant by Ingrid Bergman showing him doing his famous jig in *Indiscreet*. Even the exterior of the bungalow seemed tailor-made to suit Grant's tastes: there was a little walled-in sun deck to one side to which Grant would hasten whenever the sun came out, and where he would take off his shirt and stretch out luxuriantly in a deck chair to bring out his tan. The only problem with this, as he soon found, was that the bungalow was overlooked by the fifteen-storey, black-glass MCA Tower building that stood on the edge of the Universal lot; the spectacle of Hollywood's most glamorous leading man stripped to the waist taking the sun was too much for the hundreds of young secretaries who worked in the skyscraper. As the sun came out, they would race to the windows to see if their hero was in place. If he was, they stood and gaped; sooner or later Grant would give up and retreat indoors.

Some time passed before Weaver finally set eyes on Dyan

Cannon. A combination of his own security-conscious background and Grant's evident terror of publicity was making him almost obsessively careful about strangers. He was a little abrupt and offhand, therefore, when a tanned and composed young woman, with straight, streaked blonde hair, wearing a tennis dress and sneakers, casually pushed open the office door one afternoon and asked for Grant. Weaver stalled. 'May I ask who wants him?' The girl looked surprised and a little irritated: 'I'm Mrs Grant.' Weaver fled for the sitting room, pink with embarrassment. He had been astonished to see someone with such a natural, wholesome, unactressy appearance, with only the barest traces of make-up, more college girl than Hollywood wife.

A few months after he started working for Grant, the routine changed. *Walk, Don't Run* was finished and there was little for Grant to do at Universal, since he had no other film set up, and was showing the greatest reluctance about discussing any other movie plan with anyone. Most mornings, Weaver was now asked to come straight up to the house the Grants had rented in Benedict Canyon, some five minutes' drive from Grant's own home, but in every way larger and more suitable for a family and the staff that was now needed to look after them. This was becoming something of a pattern in Grant's life: back to his own bachelor establishment on Beverly Grove Drive, further up in the hills, and still untouched by decorators, between marriages, and then into more elegant and roomy houses with his wives. The new house which had been rented from a man called Gabor at some $2,000 a month, was a pleasant place, surrounded by eucalyptus, pine, and jacaranda trees which effectively screened it from predatory eyes, and with a pool in the middle, so that most rooms opened directly out on to the terrace and the water.

One of Weaver's first jobs at the house was a charming and absurd one, and very revealing of Grant's character. Grant hated animals and loathed all pets, but he was still extremely reluctant to hurt them. Much of the Benedict Canyon house was built of wood, however, and a woodpecker had chosen to take up residence in the roof, spending its days hammering imperiously on the walls.

Weaver, left to himself, would have made short work of the importunate bird with a pellet gun. Grant wouldn't hear of it. Instead, he instructed Weaver to try to talk the bird out of its unreasonable affection for the house,by tapping back in response to its hammerings. Duly, Weaver tapped; the woodpecker tapped back. Just as Weaver was beginning to wonder whether this might be the start of a long and time-consuming relationship, the tapping ceased. The bird had gone. Was it, Weaver wondered, that his command of woodpecker was now so fluent that he had managed to offend the bird? The joke became a bond between him and Grant.

It was now that Weaver began to realize, for the first time, that Grant was far from happy. Increasingly often, he would drive up to the house to find Grant still in his pyjamas, brooding in the room that he had turned into an office at one end of the house, ready to snarl and snap at Weaver if he said the wrong thing. Weaver would know what to expect as soon as he opened the front door: there would be an air of dither and oppression over the entire household, with the English butler Tony Faramus more sepulchral in stance and movement than ever, while the maid, another English import, tiptoed anxiously around the house, trying hard to appear invisible. Even the nanny seemed affected, so desperate to keep Jennifer silent that lines of agitation would break out across her face at the slightest whimper from the baby in its cot. The house seemed possessed of a curiously funereal air on these occasions, with the two women in their nurse-like starched white uniforms and the butler in his dark suit. It was all made even more sombre by the fact that even Weaver had been instructed by Grant to wear nothing but sober dark suits for work.

These days of rows between Grant and Dyan were a nightmare for Weaver. Grant, in his unhappiness, would settle to nothing, finding fault with his young secretary's punctuation, his prose style, even his personal habits – digressing from a letter he was dictating to lecture Weaver on the sort of food he should be eating or the way he should sit or dress. Grant himself would show little sign of wanting to get out of his pyjamas, preferring to prowl fretfully up and down the long part-office, part-bedroom that he had made into his own quarters, with its hideous bar covered in cowhide, legacy of previous tenants, jutting out into the middle of the room.

It didn't take Weaver long to find out why the Grants were fighting. Grant had never enjoyed social life, never invited friends to his house for meals, and had joined in the exotica of Hollywood life only with the most profound reluctance. True, he had good friends in the movie colony, people like Ingrid Bergman, Frank Sinatra, Gregory Peck, or Mervyn Le Roy, but he kept them at a distance, as debonair, charming, and relaxed in their company as on screen, but just as unassailable. Basically he liked to stay at home. And with a new young wife with whom he could laugh, and the baby he had always craved, he could see no reason whatsoever to go out.

Dyan, on the other hand, was barely twenty-six, a gregarious, ambitious, extremely attractive girl, who now that she had married Grant and produced a child she too doted on, wanted to have fun. For her, fun meant friends, excursions, dinner parties, and balls, and since, unlike Grant, she had nothing else to occupy her days, she needed the excitement. The subject of her work was also a prickly area in their discussions. Dyan had never really abandoned her plans to follow an acting career and now for the first time in her life she felt that she was in a position to pursue it with a certain style, not as an unknown, untried starlet begging for bit parts, but as someone of some consequence who wanted to learn how to act. Grant wanted his wife at home. He also wanted her to behave as he thought a wife should, supervising the staff, and preparing some of the meals, tending to the baby's clothes and welfare.

And so the Grants fought. Weaver, trying to merge into the background as inconspicuously as possible, could not help but overhear as he crouched over his typewriter as the two would erupt into scenes, most often sparked off by a well-meaning but tactless call from Dyan, 'Oh Cary, I'm off to acting class', at which Grant would leap to his feet to pursue her down the hall with admonitions and orders which she showed no hesitation in ignoring. With the passing weeks and growing hostility, Grant took to hiding the car keys before Dyan got up in the morning, and Dyan retaliated by jumping over the gate and making her way down to Sunset Boulevard on foot, from which she would be returned, defiant and a little sheepish, by a friend with a car later in the day. On one momentous occasion, the entire household was galvanized into appalled silence when, after a row had broken out, Grant pursued his wife into the bathroom, locked the door, and could be heard to be spanking her. A few minutes later the bathroom window was flung open and Dyan scrambled through to make her way back down the canyon and into the city.

At about this time, it became plain to everyone that help of some kind was needed if the Grants were ever going to get their relationship on a more even keel. A noted marriage guidance counsellor called Dr Andrew Salter was duly summoned to Los Angeles from New York to lend his professional touch.

The trouble was that Grant mistrusted the doctor from the start, not least because of the exorbitant scale of his fees. After sparring with him for several sessions, he had the extreme pleasure in lighting upon a weakness in the counsellor: Dr Salter was terrified of aeroplanes. From that moment on the experiment at marriage counselling was doomed. Grant used every opportunity to deflect the conversation away from the Grants and their problems in the direction of the doctor and his problems, which consisted in needling him about his phobia about flying. The doctor soon took flight and returned – by train – to New York.

The first summer of Jennifer's life was not all bad, of course. If Dyan was lonely and felt bitter about her husband's dogmatic and censorious behaviour, and if Grant despised his wife's student friends, with their flower-child attitudes and their lack of sophistication, they did at least have the baby in common, and an astonishingly privileged Hollywood baby it was too, spending its nights tucked up in an antique crib which had been handed down from one movie personality to the next, and which bore gold name-tags identifying previous occupants. Sometimes, with the child gurgling in the sunshine by the pool, a real feeling of intimacy and peace would settle over the embattled household. Then Weaver would be despatched to a Mexican take-away in San Fernando Valley and return laden with enchilladas and tacos, the sort of rich spicy food both Grants loved. For a while, tranquillity and pleasantry would reign.

And Grant could be remarkably generous towards Dyan, even if his generosity sometimes took a decidedly proprietorial form. From before the time that Weaver came to work for him, Grant had adopted the habit of getting the best New York stores to send him entire wardrobes for her on approval – dresses, suits, coats, sweaters, bags, and shoes. Weaver made the first selection and returned the bulk of the goods. Grant himself selected a number of outfits from the shortlist and the rest was sent back. The winners were then formally presented to Dyan. At no point did she ever get to see what was on offer; nor was she ever told about Grant's strange practice.

These changes of mood, Weaver soon realized, were going to be something that he would have to adjust to if he was going to survive as Grant's secretary, for they were built-in parts of his employer's personality. Always relaxed and a master of himself on screen, Grant was capable of fluctuations of temper when off it. In a very short space of time he seemed to be gripped by sudden rages and despair which would whirl in out of what looked like a serene sky, shrouding everything in uncertainty and unease, only to whisk away again as rapidly as it had appeared. It made him challenging to work for and certainly never dull, but never entirely relaxing either. Weaver was stimulated, but he was also frequently apprehensive.

Weaver soon learned that Grant noticed every detail of what went on in his household. The first few days that Weaver went up to work at Benedict Canyon he waited until Grant went off to the other end of the house to join Dyan for lunch, and then hurried down with his car into Beverly Hills, some ten minutes' drive, to get himself a sandwich. On the fourth day, he returned from his lunch to find Grant pacing impatiently up and down the office. 'There'll be no more of that,' Grant said as Weaver opened the door. 'If you're going to work for me, you work for me. You don't spend your day in Beverly Hills.' Weaver pointed out that he had been away for less than an hour. Grant paid no attention. If Weaver wanted to stay, he would have to stay at his desk all day. After that, Weaver felt that he had no choice but to collect a sandwich from a delicatessen on his way to work at eight-thirty in the morning, even though it was rubbery and dank by the time he got around to eating it, or, on the rare occasions when he was too busy to buy one, to sneak furtively into the kitchen in search of an apple or a piece of cheese, prepared, at the slightest sound of approaching footsteps, to cram the offending morsel of food into his jacket pocket. He was never invited to lunch.

It was a far more demanding job, in every way, both emotional and physical, than Weaver had ever envisaged. It had its rewards and its charms, in the shape of Grant's immensely engaging nature – when he chose to be nice – and in the variety and excitement of its tasks. Like Grant, however, Weaver seemed prone to comic and bizarre misfortunes, and these sometimes caused him to question his long-term place at Grant's side.

Much as Grant hated animals, he did, when Weaver went to work for him, own a German shepherd that had been trained as an attack dog by the army. Gumper, as the dog was called, took an immediate dislike to Weaver, and made it plain that the young secretary would not be safe if left alone with him.

One day, Tony Faramus, leaving the house on an errand, forgot to lock Gumper outside. The dog prowled down the corridor until he caught sight of Weaver, when he broke into an excited run and gave chase. The unfortunate Weaver took to his heels and escaped into a bedroom. This room gave on to an octagonal dressing room, lined with mirrors the length and breadth of every wall; unluckily, it contained a second door, through which Gumper now had the wits to enter. As Weaver reached the handle to slam it shut, he was confronted by a horrendous monster, a vision of eight snarling hounds, all in the process of tearing him to death. Unable, in his terror, to discern living dog from reflected image, Weaver turned back and just managed to reach the terrace, slamming the glass doors closed behind him before the dog sank its teeth into his leg.

Grant, when he heard the story, laughed loudly and a little maliciously at the spectacle of his somewhat stout secretary in full flight from the Hydra.

In the summer of 1966, Grant, Dyan, and the baby caught the SS *Oriana* for Southampton. It was to be a peaceful, private family outing, with a slow steam down the West Coast, through the Panama Canal, with stops at Lisbon and Le Havre. News about the trip had been kept absolutely private, the tickets had been booked in false names, and nothing had been said to anyone about the holiday.

Given the contrasting demands of the journey – high summer on a liner, a pause perhaps in France, a possibly cold and wet English summer – Dyan had spent days in Benedict Canyon agonizing about what clothes to take with her, sometimes resorting to heated arguments with Grant, who was fanatical about 'travelling light'. For once, Grant's strictures did not prevail. On the day of departure, the party – three Grants, Tony Faramus with the Rolls, Weaver with one station-wagon, a chauffeur with the other, and Grant's former agent – reached the docks at San Pedro with thirty-six suitcases. There were bags piled into boots, on back seats and car roofs: it might have been an entire tourist group preparing to emigrate to Europe.

At first, the elaborate security precautions seemed to everyone to have worked splendidly. The docks appeared deserted. But then, as Grant and Dyan, holding the baby, were climbing out of the Rolls at the foot of the gangplank, a storm exploded around them. Some 300 reporters and photographers broke out from behind distant barriers and converged on the party. People, suitcases, bags, baby equipment, passports, tickets were all swirled up in a maelstrom of shouting and hustling reporters as flashguns flared and photographers scrabbled over one another to get a closer shot.

At last, with the help of a distraught captain and a few sturdy members of the *Oriana*'s crew, the dishevelled pair with the by now howling baby were escorted on board. At one point Weaver, who had been given Dyan's jewel case to look after, dropped it, and spent a painful few minutes retrieving the Grant diamonds from among the flailing legs and kicking feet of jostling, infuriated newsmen.

On board Grant turned to vent his fury on the luckless Dyan. How could she have subjected them to all this? It was all her fault for bringing so much luggage. With which, rage growing, he began tearing open her bags, snatching out clothes – the fifty pairs of shoes she had chosen to include were a particular target for his rage – and throwing them on to the floor. Dyan burst into tears and cried mournfully. In the end, a somewhat harassed Tony Faramus was detailed to drive home to Benedict Canyon an entire station-wagon load of Dyan's clothes deemed unnecessary by Grant. A final picture of the family, caught by a *Photoplay* photographer shortly before the *Oriana* set sail, shows a slightly grim-faced Grant, lips drawn back in a perfunctory smile, while Dyan stares out, bravely but wanly. In the background stands an appalled-looking Weaver, clutching a baby's bonnet.

The Grant's marriage barely survived the triumphant trip home to present Jennifer to her eighty-eight-year-old British grandmother. On their return to Benedict Canyon Dyan moved into a minute guest house that stood by the gates. Two unhappy months dragged by while the estranged couple, fighting with ever greater bitterness, sought to settle their immense differences. By December neither had the will or the strength to go on. On the 28th, a Los Angeles newspaper carried the headline: 'Cary Grants Parted'. By then, Dyan had departed for a rented house on Malibu Beach. She had taken Jennifer with her.

5

'My Only Ticket to Eternity'

It would be hard to exaggerate what the loss of Jennifer meant to Grant. Nothing that had happened to him before, neither the disappearance of his mother when he was nine, nor the painful separation from four successive wives, seemed to have prepared him for the anguish he now suffered. Weaver, at his side during the first weeks of Dyan's departure, watched on helplessly as Grant brooded and lamented his eight-month-old baby, his moods of rage and bitterness towards Dyan gradually giving way to a permanent and profound grief.

As for Dyan, the break from Grant seemed to have transformed her life. Gone was the sulkiness, the bad temper, the sense of claustrophobia. Friends remarked that she was a totally altered person. 'I just had to get away and collect my thoughts,' she told them. 'I'm having a ball in my little apartment. I cook my own dinners – eat what I want and when I want to.' It was all a far cry from a butler, a maid, a Rolls-Royce, and the heavily guarded grandeur of Beverly Hills.

This initial sense of liberation disposed Dyan to feel generous towards her ex-husband, particularly as she was not an unkind woman and was keenly aware how much he was missing his daughter. She encouraged him to visit Jennifer whenever he wanted to. Consequently, in the bright blue, early spring Californian days that followed Dyan's departure for Malibu, Grant and Weaver would spend most afternoons on trips to the coast and back, taking it in turns to drive the Rolls or the station-wagon the ten or twelve miles down the freeway to the beach. When they got to Dyan's rented house, Grant would sit for a while with the baby, holding her on his knee, and talk to the nanny who had accompanied Dyan to Malibu, discussing with her every detail of the baby's daily progress and development. The little girl, with her beady eyes and cheerful disposition, soon took note of her father's arrivals and departures.

The visits to Malibu Beach rarely lasted very long, but Weaver noticed that they soothed Grant's misery over what had happened to him, and restored to him some sense of security about his relationship with his only child. The tranquillity of these occasions even led onlookers to speculate that the Grants might eventually reunite, a rumour which rapidly gained credence after Grant was seen at his wife's side when she took the star role in *The Ninety-Day Mistress* at the Biltmore Theater.

Friends hoping for a reconciliation were soon disappointed. As the months passed it became absolutely clear that Dyan had no intention of returning to her gilded cage, but was increasingly coming to enjoy and value the freedom of living away from Grant's watchful eye. Having first rented a house on Malibu Beach, with its floating population of divorcees, film stars and the peripatetic rich, she now bought one, savouring the colony's air of informality and the atmosphere of an endless unplanned cocktail party. Towards the end of August, some eight months after her flight from Benedict Canyon, Dyan went into the superior court in Los Angeles and sued for divorce, on the grounds that Grant had treated her in a 'cruel and inhuman' manner. In the papers she presented to the court were estimates of Grant's financial worth ('more than $10 million') and an account of her own monthly expenses, which she put at $5,470. No date for the trial of the divorce suit was set.

Postponement in these cases is usual under Californian law. The period of delay is intended to provide warring couples not so much with the opportunity for reconciliation as with the leisure to settle visitation rights and financial matters without excessive acrimony. The Grants – or rather their lawyers – spent the time rather differently, with Dyan making ever more exorbitant claims for

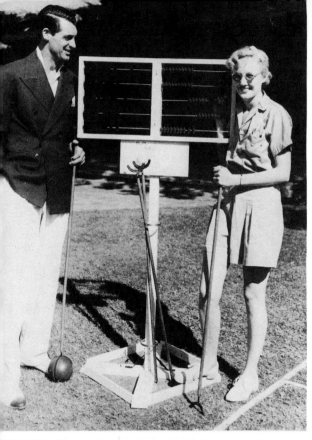

Cary Grant playing shuffle-ball at the Palm Springs Desert Inn with his first wife, Virginia Cherrill, the twice-married star of Chaplin's *City Lights* *(Rex Features)*

At the Bal Cap d'Antibes with Countess Dorothy di Frasso, the society hostess and millionairess who introduced Grant to Barbara Hutton *(Rex Features)*

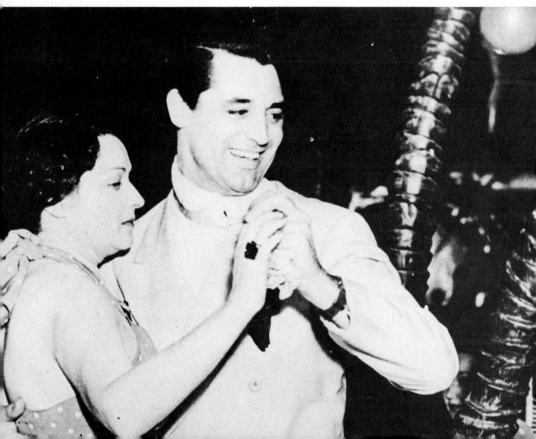

The summer of 1942, and Grant is married for the second time: to Barbara Hutton, heiress to the Woolworth fortune and rumoured to be the richest girl in the world. The gossip columns dubbed them 'Cash and Carry' *(Rex Features)*

The longest screen kiss in history: with Ingrid Bergman in Hitchcock's *Notorious*, 1946 *(RKO/courtesy of the National Film Archive Stills Library)*

Above: Grant with his third wife, Betsy Drake, the intelligent and very pretty actress Merle Oberon introduced him to on board the *Queen Mary* in 1947. As a wedding present Grant gave her a miniature poodle *(Rex Features)*

Left: With Grace Kelly in *To Catch a Thief* (1955), the film that turned her into the future Princess Grace of Monaco. It was while on location in the South of France that she met Prince Rainier *(Paramount/courtesy of the National Film Archive Stills Library)*

Below: Grant and wife number five, former public relations officer Barbara Harris, at a fashion show in New York in April 1981. Grant was seventy-seven, Barbara thirty *(Rex Features)*

Grant and Bill Weaver at work in the Beverly Grove Drive house into which they moved after the end of Grant's marriage to Dyan Cannon. Grant could be a demanding taskmaster, checking on every letter that went out *(Courtesy of* Look *magazine)*

With his fourth wife, Dyan Cannon, and a doting father at last. Grant was later to call Jennifer, born in February 1966, 'my only ticket to eternity' *(Rex Features)*

Above: Jennifer, aged three, spends a weekend with her father at Beverly Grove Drive. Bill Weaver's typewriter has been pushed to one side and father and daughter share a birthday tea at the dining-room table

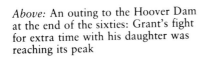

Above: An outing to the Hoover Dam at the end of the sixties: Grant's fight for extra time with his daughter was reaching its peak

Right: In a rented house in Las Vegas with Jennifer and a nanny. Grant was a frequent visitor to the city, though not to the gaming tables, enjoying the desert air and the company of old friends

Christmas 1970 at Beverly Grove Drive. A devoted father,
Grant was determined that Jennifer would not grow up spoiled
and could be firm when it came to presents and treats

Early skills: Jennifer at the blackboard in a rented house in Las Vegas. Grant preserved many of Jennifer's earliest scribblings for posterity

William McIntosh, Cary Grant and a young friend of Jennifer's sitting on the terrace of the Beverly Grove Drive house: the skyscrapers of Los Angeles stretch away below

Work begins on Grant's Shangri-la: watching excavations at
Shannonside near Kildysart in Ireland in 1973

No feature of Shannonside seemed unimportant to Grant. Here
he inspects the local livestock on one of his many walks across
the site

Shannonside rising out of the Irish mists: Grant watches as a
wall is built to surround the site of 2,100 cottages and garden
flats

Grant and McIntosh returning to New York after a tour of inspection of their Irish project. For both men, these were delightful trips, more holiday than work

Before demolition, McIntosh and Grant tour all that the old site, some 555 acres, with a former manor house, outhouses, barns and stables, possessed

1974, and the project has reached the design stage: the project
engineer, Grant and McIntosh discuss individual plans

Where the Shannon and the Fergus rivers meet: here Grant
intended to spend a tranquil old age

alimony, and with Grant arguing that he had every intention of being extremely generous, but that he still hoped for some other solution to their problems than those handed out by a formal court.

A date for the hearing was finally set for 20 March, 1968. Before defendant and plaintiff could appear in court, however, Grant was involved in a car crash on the Long Island Expressway in New York as he was leaving the city to catch a plane home from Kennedy Airport. The accident was serious: Grant's driver was very badly hurt and Grant himself was taken to St John's Hospital with bruising and grazing to his nose and mouth and three broken ribs.

In discussing the divorce with friends, Dyan had always made the assumption that her suit would not be contested and she would never be called upon to stand up in the witness box to spell out her accusations of 'cruel and inhuman' behaviour. After Grant's crash, it became widely accepted that her appearance in court would be no more than a mere formality, since Grant would now either postpone the case or agree to whatever her lawyers proposed.

As so often with Grant, public assumption of how he might behave was entirely misplaced. Grant, despite his confinement in hospital, had no intention of putting off the hearing, and none whatsoever of letting it go unchallenged. He feared Dyan's revelations, but he was still hoping that he, rather than his former wife, might be awarded eventual custody of the child. As a result, the world's press was agreeably surprised to find itself presented with a divorce case which was remarkable even in a city as notorious as Los Angeles for the spectacular nature of its divorce cases.

On 21 March, the *New York Daily News*, America's highest-circulation newspaper, carried a headline on page one: 'Life with Cary Grant a "Nightmare".' Below, in slightly smaller type: 'Wife charges he spanked her, took LSD trips.' From his hospital bed, Grant groaned. Dyan had taken off.

In the evidence that followed, America learned that Grant, the idol of millions, the leading man of impeccable morals and still more impeccable charm, was accused of being a tormentor and a tyrant in his own home. Dyan testified to the fact that Grant had

65

been taking LSD regularly, under doctor's supervision, for ten years; she called him an 'apostle' of the drug. Under its influence, she told the court, her husband had frequently beaten her. Several times, he had had 'yelling and screaming fits'. She then went on to describe an episode in which Grant, in order to prevent her from attending a friend's dinner party, took the keys to their three cars, locked the garden gates, and then shut himself up in her dressing room to read poetry. A little later, she said, 'he started to hit me, and screamed. He was laughing as he hit me, and he screamed for the help to come and see what he was doing. I was frightened because he was laughing and I went to call the police.' She had been prevented from doing so, she explained, by Grant, who pointed out to her how damaging the resulting publicity would be to all of them.

On another occasion, she told the court, when they were planning their trip to Bristol to show the new baby off to Grant's mother, Grant had refused to allow her to pack a supply of Jennifer's special baby food, saying that 'the cows in England are as good as they are in this country'.

Some of this, of course, was comic stuff, but the picture of a quirky Grant, under the influence of LSD and capable of violence, was not an edifying one. Dyan backed up her testimony with a request that Grant be allowed to have his daughter visit him only in the company of a nanny, and that these visits should never include an overnight stay.

No expense had been spared on this divorce case. Even Grant had come prepared. The previous autumn he had taken the precaution of agreeing to an examination by two psychiatrists, and these now took the stand to give their opinion that Grant was in point of fact a perfectly rational man and a competent and fit father. Dr Judd Marmor told the court that he had found no traces of bad effects from the LSD, and that he was in agreement with Grant when he told him that the drug had 'deepened his sense of compassion for people, deepened his understanding of himself, and helped cure his shyness and anxiety in dealing with other people'. Dr Sidney Pomer, the second psychiatrist, added that he had observed in Grant no evidence whatsoever of 'irrationality, erratic behaviour, or incoherence'. Through them, Grant reasoned that he had spanked Dyan for 'reasonable and adequate causes'.

The next day, 21 March, Judge Robert A. Wenke rose to deliver his verdict. It was less harsh on Grant than some of his friends had feared. Dyan was granted her divorce, but her alimony was set at $50,000 a year – somewhat less than she had asked for – and Grant was awarded two months each year for 'visitation', with none of Dyan's restrictions about nannies or overnight stays, because the judge said that he fully believed the evidence put before him that the actor had not used LSD in over a year.

Sensational trials are commonplace in Hollywood. Even the sort of disclosures that Dyan had chosen to make about Grant's personal habits made a remarkably small dent on the public's image of their favourite star. They had weathered three of his previous divorces: what was so very different about a fourth? In any case, gossip columnists have notoriously short memories, and there were soon other Hollywood divorces, every bit as juicy and newsworthy, to distract them. As David Shipman, author of a book on the Hollywood stars, remarked: 'more than any other star he belonged to the public. When his fourth wife divorced him and in court did a thorough character assassination job on him, no one cared, no one was interested. They looked the other way.'

Grant's own comment on the whole affair could well have come straight from the mouth of any one of his smoother male parts: 'Once the female has used the male for procreation,' he remarked wryly, 'she turns on him and literally devours him.'

Once the divorce was concluded, the Grants quickly settled down to the routine of shared parental duties usual to most divorced families, the difference being, perhaps, the degree of passion that Grant, as father, brought to his small and only daughter, unexpected in most men, and exceptional indeed in a four-times married sixty-three-year-old Hollywood star. There were rows and complications between Dyan and Grant over visitation hours, mismanaged plans, and broken promises, certainly, and many times the two had to return to court for further arbitration of their differences, but some form of *modus vivendi* was gradually established. 'You get desperate to see your child, absolutely desperate,' Grant would explain to friends when they questioned him, slightly perplexed, about the tenacity with which he seemed to pursue his rights as father. For he definitely pursued them, every one of them, counting the days allocated to him with almost fanatic eagerness, and jealously monitoring every hour Jennifer spent with him.

Grant, Weaver soon observed, was not a very relaxed father. He doted on the child, but he had, hardly surprisingly, given his age and the absence of all children in his life hitherto, little natural aptitude with young children. When Jennifer, as she began to toddle, grew fretful, her father was liable to turn bored and restless. In this, however, Grant was fortunate in his selection of secretary, for Weaver, along with his commercial skills and his ability to drive a Rolls and carry suitcases, was also a willing and practised child-minder, having looked after five brothers and sisters when his stepfather died. After the dissolution of his marriage, Grant had moved out of Benedict Canyon and returned to Beverly Grove Drive, and Weaver now recruited his younger brother, David, to act as houseman for the family, Tony Faramus having departed some months earlier. David, barely sixteen, was naturally affectionate and easy with children. Between the three of them – Grant, in his sixties, and the two young men – caring for Jennifer became an adventure, an experience to anticipate and enjoy, particularly as she brought with her each time a nanny who did the actual work, leaving the entertainment and the fun to the three men.

It was certainly fun, but in those early days at least there was a lot of experimenting to be done. Grant, for instance, had never celebrated Christmas. He treated the whole occasion precisely as he treated any other day, and had done so since childhood. Weaver, on the other hand, felt that the child's first formal Christmas with her father should be as like that of other children as possible, complete with stocking, Father Christmas, and Christmas lunch. He even volunteered to cook the turkey himself. A reusable plastic Christmas tree was bought at Zody's, a local discount store, presents were organized, including nuts, fruit, and an autographed picture of himself in a Cartier frame. After much planning and discussion a fully fledged Christmas took shape, the final touch being the triumphant carving of the turkey, though that came about only as a result of Weaver's coaxing, having persuaded his employer to drop in on the canteen at Universal and take a lesson in carving from the chef. (After the carving lesson, Grant tipped him $100; the electric carving knife, 'purchased' on a trial basis for the occasion, was sent back to the shop two days after Christmas, and a refund handed over, all part of Grant's extraordinarily paradoxical attitude towards money.)

Not long after retreating back to his bachelor quarters up the canyon, Grant agreed to have a corner of his house turned into a bedroom for Jennifer. Dyan had been objecting to the way that the little girl shared her father's bedroom – and, usually, his bed – when she came to stay with him, and had been threatening to make Grant return to the courts to settle the dispute. Grant gave in.

It was typical of him, loath as he was to tinker with any other part of his increasingly dishevelled and dilapidated house, that he now agreed to bring in Bob Baldwin, the artist who had decorated his bungalow at Universal, to cover Jennifer's walls and furniture with *trompe-l'oeil* designs, picturing little joke toys, fruit, and cascading bunches of flowers. On her chest of drawers, Baldwin painted a couple of dolls, one with her hand mysteriously stretched around a drawer, the other ostensibly hanging from a knob. The effect was charming and Grant supervised each of the details with almost obsessive care.

When Jennifer had turned three months, Phillipe Halsman, a noted French photographer, had been invited to California to take the first official picture of the baby. Now that she was growing up, Grant turned court photographer himself, devoting hours of the precious visits to crouching behind the camera, watching Jennifer at play, or taking snaps of all her toys, so as to chronicle, for later on, the mementoes of childhood.

This desire not to miss out on a single stage or nuance of his daughter's babyhood became something of an obsession with Grant, who soon took to wearing the child's first lost tooth, shed happily during one visit to the house, from a gold chain hung around his neck, encased in a little lucite locket. All Jennifer's scribblings were preserved for posterity. Some of the very first were even transferred on to a set of plates which Grant kept stacked up in the dining room. 'Look at these pictures,' he would say to visitors. 'You don't see any turned-down mouths. Everyone's smiling and the sun is out. Won't they be wonderful to serve lunch on?'

Grant was indeed a doting father, even an excessively doting one, but he was not, as Weaver observed, a spoiling one. It was perhaps because he remembered the attention to manners that his own parents had insisted on that he demanded such politeness of his own daughter, particularly towards guests or staff. William Currie McIntosh, a business friend of Grant's who got to know the family at about this time, remembers an enchanting little girl, with her mother's fine blonde hair and long lashes, and her father's dimpled chin (also her father's long slender arms), ever quick to thank him for small presents he brought to the house. Nor did Jennifer have more than the ordinary child's wardrobe.

In these first few years, as Jennifer turned from baby to toddler, from toddler to small girl, the regular visits to her father's house in Beverly Hills never lost their extraordinary charm. Some days the entire party would go off to have tea, muffins, and cakes in an old English tea room in Santa Monica. Others, Grant would arrange for his private plane to take them to nearby Catalina Island, where they would lunch on fresh fish in a little restaurant overlooking the harbour and the casino.

Grant did not always go along on every excursion. When Halloween came round, Weaver would take the little girl 'trick or treating' round Beverly Hills with Terry Moore and her children. It was on these outings that Weaver discovered that Jennifer had inherited at least one pronounced characteristic of her father: she was immensely attractive to strangers. One day Weaver and his brother David took her to Brentwood Market in search of Easter egg colouring with which to paint eggs for the coming holiday. As they had paused and were sitting on a bench, an elegant, exquisitely dressed woman came up and sat next to Jennifer, remarking to Weaver on the child's charm and good looks. It was Nancy Reagan, who, when Weaver told her, was astonished to learn that this was Jennifer Grant, daughter of her old friend Cary.

It was not always a question of treats. Often Grant and his daughter would spend their day quietly at home, with Grant stretched out in the sunshine and Jennifer dipping in the pool, with meals served to them on trays which they ate lying on Grant's immense bed, more informal and infinitely more fun for the little girl.

When she started attending regular school, Buckley, a private school in Van Nuys, the school bus route chanced to pass by Grant's house. Grant detailed Weaver and his brother to watch out across the canyon each morning and evening for the familiar bright yellow coach and, as it approached the house, the bus, by agreement with the driver, would stop, and Grant and his daughter would exchange affectionate greetings. Sometimes Grant would have a little present waiting for her; in return, Jennifer presented him with her drawings or paper chains.

As she grew older, Jennifer started begging to be allowed to have a pet. She asked for a dog, a cat, even a rabbit. Grant, always a little squeamish about household animals, refused. Instead, he offered to find her a horse, and soon accepted, from a breeder friend, the gift of an Apaloosa for Jennifer to ride. The horse was kept stabled in Malibu Colony, and as Jennifer grew more assured so Grant would join her whenever he could and the two would go riding along the beach.

Apaloosas, however, are highly strung beasts and the mount proved too frisky for a beginner. Weaver, whose father had been a jockey, knew something about horses and he went one day to visit a children's camp not far outside Los Angeles where horses were specially trained for child riders. Here Grant bought his daughter a gentle, dun-coloured retired circus horse, which went to join its more lively predecessor in Malibu Colony.

Horseback riding in Grant's eyes was an acceptable pursuit and he didn't even object when his daughter insisted on adopting

71

Western rather than British style; more comfortable, but decidedly less classy. Other activities which Jennifer longed to take up were not so welcome to her father. It may have been because of Grant's own past, deprived of each and every one of these activities, that he had developed over the years an extremely clear idea of just what constituted in his eyes a 'respectable' sport and what did not. Bowling, ice and roller skating, for example, were out; skiing and tennis were in. Jennifer, who was athletic and lithe, like both her parents, with some of Grant's old acrobatic suppleness, took naturally to all of them, but rather less naturally to the piano lessons that Grant arranged for her to take, hoping that she might share some of the casual fun he himself had with the instrument.

That Jennifer was able to live such a normal life, and turn into such an extremely likeable and normal child, says much for the determination of both parents that their only child should not be handicapped by their differences. Jennifer also had a good deal to contend with, simply because Grant was the star that he was. There was, for instance, the ever present risk of kidnapping, which meant that Grant was adamant that his house, especially the interior, should never be photographed or described, thereby providing trespassers with information about its layout. (He could do nothing about the Map of the Stars' Homes, a street guide to the houses of the Hollywood celebrities, designed for tourists and on sale in most gift shops in Los Angeles.)

On the whole, despite the extra vigilance, Grant did manage to allow Jennifer the semblance of normality, even if the question of security took on added importance after Sharon Tate was found murdered in her home scarcely half a mile, as the crow flies, from Grant's house. Grant was away at the time, but Weaver was in residence. Within minutes of the mutilated bodies being discovered, the canyons behind Beverly Hills were crawling with security firm contractors, installing new barbed wire fences, electronic devices, and alarm systems. By the time Jennifer next came to stay, her little friend up the hill was guarded by three Alsatians, most householders had bought themselves guns, and a new mood of anxiety seemed to have gripped the valleys. Grant, despite finding that his name had been on Manson's hit list, appeared curiously cool about the whole business. He tightened up the more obvious chinks in the security provisions of the house but insisted that it should not be made to resemble Fort Knox, on the grounds that it was unnecessarily alarming to the child.

The danger of a terrorist or maniac assault was in fact probably far less real than that of Jennifer being smothered by the press.

Whatever he did, wherever he went, Grant was news. And what more attractive spectacle than that of capturing a picture of father and daughter together? Grant, ever plagued by photographers when on his own, was triply plagued if he set foot outside the gates of Beverly Drive clasping a small child by the hand. An attempted visit to Disneyland taught him a lesson he never forgot.

Grant, Jennifer, and Weaver arrived at the gates of Disneyland late one morning, intending to spend a leisurely day showing the little girl the sights. Instantly crowds gathered to gape, touch, jostle, admire. Grant, who had anticipated such a reaction, had warned the Disneyland manager of their impending visit, and the staff hastened out to gather the party inside unharmed.

Once through the barrier, Grant went to considerable lengths to remain anonymous. He kept his head well down, his neck sunk low inside his collar, and one hand half concealing his face. He tried to adopt an unsmiling, unapproachable expression. His ruse came to nothing. One woman, advancing towards the party, guessed who he was, gave up all her earlier plans to visit Disneyland, and devoted her afternoon instead to the far more enjoyable task of making the Grants' life a misery. As they walked along, she circled round them, coming in closer and closer like a predatory scavenger.

Finally, still keeping his temper, but by now decidedly harassed, Grant decided to lose his importunate tail by taking refuge for a while in the men's restroom. The woman followed at his heels to the very door, then faltered and turned back. But by now other onlookers had picked up the scent, and a man watching by the entrance called out excitedly: 'Aren't you Cary Grant?' It was the sort of question the wry, self-deprecating leading man could handle to perfection. 'I'm not really sure,' he replied courteously, 'because

I'm not myself today.' It was Grant parodying himself. The line came straight from *Bringing up Baby*, the 1938 Howard Hawks film in which Grant and Katharine Hepburn found themselves in charge of a pet leopard.

The constant background to Jennifer's pleasant visits to her father these first years was a nasty, bitter wrangle between her parents, which smouldered on month after month. Dyan had declared war on the day of the divorce hearing with her courtroom revelations; Grant, who never abandoned hope of gaining custody of the child, fought back, doggedly, year after year – guerilla skirmishes designed to wear the opposition into submission. He fought over Jennifer's schools (Dyan favoured a progressive education, Grant a studious one); he fought over possessions (when Dyan took to making unannounced raids on the house in the hopes of retrieving some of the more sumptuous wedding presents, Grant got Weaver to hide them in the foundations of the house. To escape Dyan's tirades, he locked himself in the bathroom); he fought over vacations and over houses. (He had rented a house of his own on Malibu Beach, a couple of houses along the beach from Dyan's, so as to be able to spend more time with his daughter: Dyan protested loudly that this came under the heading of spying.) And she complained in court that Grant kept watching Jennifer through binoculars when she was playing volley-ball on the beach.

Not long after her departure to Malibu – which Grant referred to as the most expensive slum in America – Grant arranged to have Dyan watched by a private detective. The intention, he told his friend William McIntosh, was to make absolutely certain that her household was a suitable establishment in which to raise Jennifer. The detective returned with tales of late-night parties, of marijuana, of chaos, with meals cooked at random and eaten in confusion. Dyan, it was clear at one point, was taking drugs, and finding it extremely hard to manage her own life in a coherent fashion. On one visit, the detective found her living in one room in Big Sur, with fourteen people.

Grant, who brooded over these reports, worrying deeply about the effect all this could have on Jennifer, might well have used them against Dyan in court, but inevitably, at the last minute, he would shy away from doing so, largely because he didn't want to blacken Dyan's character in Jennifer's eyes, and knew only too well the reaction of the press towards any public revelations of this kind. At one point, however, he grew so agitated about what might be going on in Jennifer's mind as a result of her strange life that he took to planting tape-recorders around the house and in her bedroom when she came to spend a night, hoping that they might pick up some of her feelings towards Dyan or towards himself when she talked to friends she brought home to play. The tapes revealed nothing, but they did upset Jennifer. When she discovered one hidden in her room, she said miserably to Weaver as he drove her to school one morning: 'Oh, Bill, I wonder if he's got a recorder in the car too?'

Grant was never really prepared to play any kind of dirty game in court; it was neither his nature nor his style. He was, on the other hand, determined to keep a vigilant eye on every possible legal loophole, and time after time the Grants returned to the courts with some fresh petition from him, some weary counter-attack from her. Grant lost them all. In 1971 he brought a suit against Dyan, claiming that his ex-wife had not established a home in California, and was therefore in violation of the divorce settlement. He lost that one too.

But then in 1973, when Jennifer was six, he scored at least a minor victory. Dyan had applied to the court to be allowed to take Jennifer with her to New York where she was to spend three months working on a film with Burt Reynolds. (She needed the judge's permission: by now Grant had obtained at least an order that Jennifer could not be taken out of the state of California without a court order.) To everyone's surprise, Judge Jack T. Ryburn, of Los Angeles superior court, ruled that she couldn't and awarded Grant three months' full custody of the child. It was a glorious summer up in the Beverly Grove Drive house, even though a boat trip to Alaska had to be postponed at the last minute, when *Time* magazine printed a photograph of the Grants turning up to collect their ticket; Grant feared a repeat of the Disneyland experience. Instead, they rented a cabin on a dude ranch on the edge of the desert and rode.

The point about these years – the ones of Jennifer's infancy and her father's sixties, a time of life when most men are slowing down but which for Grant appeared unmarked by the process of ageing – was that they were the best thing that had ever happened to him. He had never in his life been as happy as during the time he now spent with Jennifer. 'If I had known all my life what I now know,' he would say to friends, 'I would have had a hundred children and built a ranch to keep them on.' Of course, there were fights, but these were the normal tantrums of childhood and neither Grant nor Jennifer suffered from them.

So paramount was she in his life that Grant never showed the slightest hesitation in refusing or cancelling engagements, however prestigious or entertaining, once he had made a plan with Dyan to see his daughter. One weekend, in the early 1970s, when Dyan suddenly switched round weekends at the last moment, Grant good-humouredly gave up some ring-side seats he had been given for the presidential inauguration. 'That's all right,' he told McIntosh cheerfully over the telephone. 'I'll be with my child, which is more important. And I can see it all on television.'

Some time later he was asked to appear at the United Nations salute to the people of Bristol who had been bombed during the Second World War. Grant, who happened to have Jennifer with him at the time, caught a late flight to New York one evening, arrived early next morning, appeared at the UN for the one-hour tribute, then flew straight back to Los Angeles where, thanks to the difference in time, he arrived at the right moment to pick her up from school. These meetings with his daughter were sacred: nothing, ever, was allowed to interfere with them.

The love he felt towards this only child of his later life seemed, to close friends, to mellow the actor and to provide him with a new outlook on his entire existence. He seemed to go back over the priorities he had long accepted and now came up with different answers and solutions. To people who asked him what he wanted for her future, he would say: 'I pray she will get married and have children. I want her to give one man love and confidence and help. It has taken me many years to learn that. I was playing a different game entirely. My wives and I were never one. We were competing. I will advise Jennifer to love someone and be loved. Anything else she may get in her life is a bonus.'

Jennifer was his bonus; and she had come, by supreme good fortune, at the very moment in his life when he could most enjoy her. Often, to friends, he spoke of her as 'my only ticket to eternity'.

6

Mr Blandings Builds His Dream House

Cary Grant was not unique in his peculiar ambivalence towards his home. Many others before and since have suffered from unexplained phobias in which they feel a need to keep building, and an equally powerful one never to complete the project they have embarked on. Jane Ellen Winchester, widow of the inventor of the Winchester rifle, once constructed an enormous mansion with staircases leading to nowhere and doors opening onto nothing. Psychiatrists have suggested that this frenzied pattern of advance and retreat is no more than a reaction to the fear of dying, as if the completion of a building represents some form of death.

Grant never seemed to show any particular or exaggerated fear of dying, but the contradictory and unhappy behaviour he demonstrated over the very bricks and mortar of his house on Beverly Grove Drive was extraordinary in a man outwardly so serene. To Weaver, who was an intimate observer of the move back from Benedict Canyon, and who watched Grant's uncertainties and changes of mood, sometimes from hour to hour, this house seemed to become a vivid expression of Grant's inner turmoil, the single most revealing side of a character marked by extreme paradox, but so closely guarded as to allow very few chinks. Dithering over his house in the late 1960s and early 1970s became an acceptable outlet for Grant's pent-up confusions; he let them ride to the full.

Beverly Grove Drive had once belonged to Howard Hughes. Both the millionaire aviator and Katharine Hepburn, who used the house for a while later, valued it for its privacy, the feeling it conferred upon its inhabitants that they were somehow inviolate, perched out over the canyon beyond reach of prying eyes. There was nothing geographically remote about the plot of land on which it stood, some ten minutes' drive up into the hills behind the centre of Beverly Hills. But the fact that it was reached down a driveway, away from a corner, on a very zigzaggy, almost mountainous road, and that once inside the house, or standing out on the terrace, nothing could be seen of mankind beyond a few other one-storey houses, similarly isolated, and equally shrouded in greenery, clinging to other slopes on the far side of the canyon, meant that an occupant could pretend that he was many miles away in the mountains.

True, the orange lights of Los Angeles glowed out after dark far below in the plain, stretching almost as far as the eye could see down to the ocean, but they only seemed to enhance a feeling of remoteness. No actual person was often visible, however diminished by distance, in any direction whatsoever. Even the kidney-shaped swimming pools, dotted in the valley below, seemed scarcely to be used, their rich and elderly Beverly Hills owners preferring the tranquillity of their patios, and so they glittered, brilliantly blue and undisturbed, like far-off duck ponds. The stillness of the canyon on any one of the clear Californian mornings was intense.

During Grant's marriage to Dyan Cannon, the bachelor house had rarely been used, other than occasionally by Tony Faramus, the English butler. Since no repairs of any kind had been done to the house for many years, its state of dereliction was almost beyond description when Grant finally decided to return home in the early spring of 1967. A visitor needed to step no further than the entrance before witnessing chaos: both the screen-door to the house and the trellis-work breezeway which joined the garage to the main house had collapsed. The roof was in the same sort of condition. Grant and Weaver moved back in the middle of rain and storms. During the first few nights Weaver had to clamber up on to the tiles in driving rain to lay out squares of heavy plastic over the holes, securing them in place with logs of wood intended for the open fire.

(One night, there was a minor earthquake: as Grant and Weaver hurried out of the house to get into the open, the logs hurtled down on to their heads.)

Inside, the same decay was apparent in every room. Water stains had pitted the ceiling, where entire patches of plaster sagged dangerously under the weight of water collecting in the eaves. In the bathroom, whenever it rained hard, a rivulet of water streamed down from the central overhead light fitting.

Grant was not greatly perturbed by the ramshackle nature of his house. He organized Weaver into positioning empty jam jars and paint tins under the most serious of the drips, and then set about sifting through the old and by now very soggy cartons of his belongings that were piled on top of each other in every available free corner. He was even rather pleased when the county came to inspect his property and declared themselves so appalled by the rotting vegetation that they placed a lien on it until the weeds were cut. Since he refused to get the work contracted the county sent a team of Mexican labourers to cut back the jungle that threatened to engulf the estate. The fact that labourers had been sent in, Grant explained to Weaver, was an excellent solution to the problem; it meant that he would have to spend far less than he would have had to pay for a proper Beverly Hills' gardener to do the same work.

The attitude of the city authorities – bemused by the actor's eccentricity, perturbed at the potential damage it might cause – was, in fact, rather entertaining to Grant. It was only when, not long after he had moved back, the city issued him with an ultimatum of either getting the house entirely remodelled or having the property condemned that he agreed to take the subject at all seriously. Even so, ten years were to elapse before a completed house, largely rebuilt and totally redecorated, was to rise up out of the ashes of the old, and much of those ten years was spent in an elaborate, costly, and time-consuming game involving architects and surveyors, lawyers and inspectors, builders and painters.

In the first few months following the city's ruling on his property, Grant entered into the project of restoration with a certain amount of vigour. He engaged an architect to draw up plans, initially only for an extra room for Jennifer, with a token gesture towards repairing the rest of the house. But as work on that room began, so he indulged in day-dreams and even architectural drawings for the next, plans constantly revised, swapped, or supplanted by new ideas. Beverly Grove Drive became a perpetual building site and a scene of constant comedy routine, reminding Weaver strongly of H.C. Potters' *Mr Blandings Builds His Dream House* in which Grant grappled with the snares of home-ownership. As if in daily self-parody, Grant never failed to trip over the runner of the sliding doors that led to the terrace, stubbing his toes and letting out curses of rage. (There was, however, one compensation. It was not a shrine, as the Benedict Canyon house had been. At some point on one of their tours of America the Beatles had briefly come to rest in the Gabor house. For months after Grant had rented it, fans, ignorant of their departure, continued to besiege the property. On occasion Weaver would find their pale faces pressed enquiringly to the window panes. The more persistent, who had braved a hair-raising climb up an almost sheer precipice covered in spiky brushwood, would have to be hosed off the premises.)

To match the architectural fervour that was going on, Grant got Weaver to start some constructive household project of his own. One day, searching through the garage for a hammer, he had chanced upon several rusty and ancient cans full of old nails. He had carried them indoors with an air of triumph and asked Weaver to comb through them and sort them out into matching sizes and shapes. This done, he was sent off down into Beverly Hills to find appropriate containers to store them in, and later to find particular kinds of label to identify them with. Grant viewed the scheme with considerable pleasure: it seemed to him to combine good sense with thriftiness.

With time, the appearance of the house slowly began to improve. Jennifer's new room, when freshly decorated, encouraged Grant to keep going. Weaver helped the process along by volunteering to sort through the rotting cardboard boxes, still sitting piled up along the corridors. One of the problems was that the French doors leading out on to the terrace had become so warped with the rain that cracks had developed in the wood, large enough to put a hand through and certainly large enough to allow generous streams of water to form rivers along the flagstone floor. The boxes, when Weaver broached them, were disintegrating, the papers dank and mildewed, with a pervading smell of must. Among the books and papers he unearthed were the two Tiepolo sketches that Barbara Hutton had given Grant so many years before. These he now urged Grant to donate to the Los Angeles County Museum of Art fearing for their preservation and Grant agreed – a bonus resulting from his gift was $35,000 apiece in tax credits. The Boudin painting, also sitting propped up among the soaking debris of Grant's past, was salvaged and hung from a nail in the sitting room. Furniture was brought in from the old bungalow at Universal, including the bright yellow Mexican table and, as the architects and builders made progress with the roof and walls, so Grant commissioned new *trompe-l'oeil* painting for his bedroom, more brown leather furniture, and a great deal more yellow and white canvas for curtains.

None of this work, however, was accomplished without legal bickerings, ill feelings and constant alteration of plans. Some of it, unquestionably, came from Grant himself, who now as never before revealed the extent of the indecisiveness of his nature. Two electricians spent an entire day, earning $20 an hour each, changing the position of a single light socket five times. Finally, scarcely able to keep their tempers under control, they asked Grant to draw an X in pencil precisely where he wanted it.

Doubtless in part because he attracted this kind of misfortune, Grant was also plagued by a succession of unscrupulous contractors and poor workmen. He was vulnerable to them, largely because he had such very clear ideas – even though he kept changing them – of how things should look. The results, good or bad, in any case rarely came up to his expectations.

The first disaster to strike Beverly Grove Drive concerned a set of specially commissioned tiles. Behind the house stood a fan-shaped, semi-circular patio and for this Grant had ordered a selection of tiles, constructed out of a special clay, to be fired in the

83

precise sizes and shapes to fit the exact contours of the terrace.

The tiles were to be transported by truck from Mexico, where they were baked, to Beverly Hills. Enormous care had gone into the packing of the load, each tile placed in such a way as to fit most easily into the architect's design once they reached Grant's house. A good deal of straw had been laid between each piece, as padding to prevent breakage. Somewhere along the journey, the driver of the truck, his mind on other matters, tossed the butt of his cigarette over his shoulder and in to the dry straw, where it exploded instantly into flames. He was an enterprising fellow, however, and managed to extinguish the fire, leaving the tiles scorched and blackened on one side, but not cracked. On arriving in Beverly Hills, he hastily unloaded the truck, depositing the tiles good side up with the more marked ones at the bottom of the pile, and vanished away again down the road before either Grant or Weaver took in what had happened.

After that, came the saga of the plaster. The contractor in charge of building, thinking to save money, used an over-generous proportion of sand in his cement. He also chose to carry out the work of replastering a wall during a full-blown Santa Anna wind, when the Mohave desert funnels its hot, dry breezes straight into the Los Angeles basin. The combination meant that the plaster, in any case too friable, dried too quickly, and no sooner was one wall completed than the entire surface erupted into cracks, both horizontal and vertical, giving an effect, within minutes, of an enormous black-and-white chequerboard. The contractor claimed that it was all an act of God. Grant sued.

After this, a bronze canopy intended to cover a small terrace outside Grant's bedroom was welded inside out, in such a way that ribs and rivets were clearly visible; then the new plumbing was connected to ancient pipes, thereby causing a flood of leaks and blockages; finally, the brackets around a theatrical mirror in Grant's bedroom were screwed in so tightly that the entire framework exploded. And so the mishaps went on; it seemed, sometimes, that Howard Hughes' old home was jinxed.

Nor were matters improved by Grant's fanaticism when it came to detail. Immense plate-glass windows, fourteen feet wide and arched at the top, had been planned for the sitting room, to give a 180-degree unobstructed view of the city below. Everyone involved with the house scoured the United States for a glass foundry able to manufacture a pane this size and shape without partitions. Not one could be found. A foundry in France agreed to take on the job, but then, dismayed by the challenge, backed out. Finally an American contractor accepted, provided they could break the window up into three separate panes, using divider posts. Some months later, the vast panes, ferried at immense cost across the continent, arrived. The effect was perfect, except in one respect; down in the very bottom left-hand corner, virtually imperceptible to the naked eye, was the manufacturer's logo. Grant had the panes removed.

Some of the mishaps, particularly those of Grant's making, took decidedly comic turns. At times like these, Beverly Grove Drive assumed the appearance of a Buster Keaton movie set.

It had been decided, early on in conversations with the architects, that a vast jacaranda tree that grew on the front lawn would have to be removed to make way for the various extensions planned for the house. Estimates for the job of cutting it down were obtained from local lumberjacks, but Grant pronounced them all too high. 'We'll handle this ourselves,' he said to Weaver. 'I know just what to do.'

Weaver was then despatched to buy a large electric chain-saw and thick jute ropes (between the two, the bill was not far short of the lowest lumberjack's estimate) which David, his brother, and he attached to the base of the jacaranda, leaving one end free to tie to the mudguard of the station-wagon. The intention was for David to drive the car up the hill in the direction they wanted the jacaranda to fall, once Weaver had gone to work with the electric saw.

The trouble was that neither man had ever cut down a tree before. Oblivious to the fact that trees, when chopped, fall on the side on which they are cut, Weaver kept wedging the tree on the opposite side. Meanwhile he worked away hard at the trunk with his chain-saw. When the tree started groaning and creaking, intimating that it was on the verge of coming down, he hurried round to the back and gestured to David to start up the car. David did so and began to pull away, whereupon, with a loud tearing noise, the rope snapped, and the tree, like an immense pea-shooter, catapulted off in the opposite direction, heading down the valley and dragging with it electricity wires, a white fence, and two avocado trees, which sent an abundant crop of their ripe fruit bouncing and cascading over the rocks as they plummeted into the canyon below.

As the house gradually began to take shape about him, and became habitable to the point that Grant and Weaver did not have to devote their entire time to minor household repairs or salvage operations, so Grant seemed, little by little, to relax. Ever a man of routine, he took to organizing his days with all the old precision that he had brought to life on the Universal lot in the mid-1960s. It was a routine marked by conscientiousness, attention to detail, a certain amount of fretfulness – and foibles.

Grant woke extremely early in the mornings. Weaver could hear him pacing around the corridors not long after dawn in search of distraction. At 6 a.m. coffee and the newspapers would be placed outside his bedroom door. Weaver felt called upon to rise early, a practice made all the easier by Grant's tendency to come creaking along the passage outside his bedroom, making what noise he could, to ensure that his young secretary did not linger long in his bed. While he ate breakfast, usually still stretched out on his bed wearing pyjamas and a champagne silk dressing gown specially made for him by a man's designer in Tokyo, Grant would go through the papers, marking items he wished to have on record.

By 9 a.m., Grant would be ready for the day, dressed in his invariable slacks and turtle-neck sweater – or a shirt if the day was hot – and impatient to get down to work. This meant long telephone calls, to business colleagues, or to Stanley Fox, his attorney, or, frequently, to the architects and builders currently in the process of doing something drastically wrong to the house. There would be lengthy arguments.

Grant received dozens of invitations a day – to dinner parties, to gala openings, to charity performances, to previews, to fund-raising events. It was very rare for him to agree to attend any of them, and he complained over the phone to friends like William McIntosh that: 'There's a banquet every night. Every bloody night out here. There's one for Bob Hope, one for Jack Benny, one for every guy in the world. You can't do them all. I'd rather dine quietly down on the beach.' He neither wanted to go nor really ever wished to be invited again, but he insisted always on the most punctilious and courteously phrased refusals. Every letter and envelope written by Weaver was scrutinized by Grant, who had decreed that no sentence was to end with the word 'I', and that the names and addresses on the envelopes had to be typed in capital letters. When they were ready for his signature, he checked them.

Correspondence took most of the morning. The many letters received by William McIntosh show how perceptive and witty a letter-writer Grant was. Then came sunbathing and lunch, eaten usually on the terrace, still tanning, and it consisted almost invariably of English muffins with melted cheese and Worcestershire sauce, or bacon and eggs and toast, and tea, drunk plain. Grant loved all food commonly associated with breakfast. Then followed a desultory afternoon, perhaps a little piano playing, maybe some more telephoning to friends, or another stint by the pool catching the sun. Never in the water however: Grant played no sports and took no physical exercise of any kind, other than his occasional rides with Jennifer, a remarkable fact given his extremely healthy and athletic appearance. If he felt a bit out of shape, he simply ate and drank a little less for a few days. Occasionally after lunch there would be visitors, perhaps a divorce attorney, with whom Grant would discuss the endless litigations with Dyan Cannon over custody, or an architect bringing a blueprint for inspection. Grant had become extremely knowledgeable about architect's plans and drawings and extremely specific in his instructions. He had, for instance, a mania about wood, and spent many hours selecting between different woods one most suitable for his bookcases.

During all this time, while Grant talked or phoned or prowled about in his restless way, Weaver would get down to the most irritating and time-consuming of his chores: the filing. One of Grant's manias was clipping stories out of newspapers and having them meticulously filed away, in boxes, packing chests, and later specially designed filing cabinets. Some of these were stories about himself that had appeared in newspapers; others were items he considered might one day come in useful. He demanded that he should be able to have them all to hand, so as to be able to rootle about through them in the loneliness and boredom of the early mornings. (Barbara Hutton once complained that Grant was far more interested in his old clippings than he was in her, and Betsy Drake told friends that she had to phone Grant by internal telephone from her own bedroom in the early mornings to see whether she could come and see him. 'Not yet,' Grant would often say, 'I'm busy.')

To handle the voluminous and fast-growing collection of fading newspaper stories Weaver had to design a comprehensive filing system, running from 'Automobile to Zebra', with many sub-categories and cross-references, the most ludicrous of which, he felt, were the categories given over to 'special offers' which Grant, perched triumphantly on his bed with his pair of scissors, would carefully cut out, morning after morning.

He never did anything with them at the time, other than draw Weaver's attention to offers as inappropriate to Grant's life as they were unnecessary – do-it-yourself gadgets, unfinished furniture. But years later, going through the boxes, he would suddenly light upon an item and pull it out, fully confident that the store in question would still be selling off 'three sweat shirts for the price of one' or an 'occasional table slightly damaged' that he had suddenly decided he badly needed.

Early on in his marriage to Betsy Drake, Grant had set himself the rule of never having a drink before six-thirty in the evening. Once installed back in Beverly Grove Drive with Weaver he kept rigidly to his timetable, refusing all alcohol until the moment that he decreed that a vodka and orange juice should be brought to him. By this time of day, when he was alone, he was often back in his bedroom once more, not in bed, but lying on it, surveying a room that he had decided to decorate in various shades of green, with bookshelves on either side of the bed, a brown leather headboard, and a painting of two Mexican children awake but in bed. The evenings were given over to television, of which Grant was a very restless viewer, keeping his hand on the remote control and switching across every couple of minutes to a new channel. When an old movie that he had appeared in came on, he would call Weaver to join him and they would watch it together, laughing enjoyably. Dinner, too, was served in bed. Plain food, with a sweet dessert, for Grant had a love of sweet food.

Grant, Weaver noticed, read very little and, when he did, it was never fiction, but biography and some current affairs. He listened to little music, though the house was full of gramophones and tape-recorders, but he did spend a great deal of time on his clothes. Having been, for many years, on the list of the Ten Best-Dressed Men in the world, he was extremely conscious of what he wore, of what suited him and what did not. By the time Weaver came to work for him, Grant had long since perfected a style of his own, with high armpits to his jackets and alterations done to very detailed specification. He was not easily swayed by moods of fashion, preferring to stick to proven, and usually rather conservative, styles that he knew, with certainty, showed him off to perfection.

His sweaters came from N. Peal, in the Burlington Arcade in London, where he also went to buy jackets from Aquascutum. In Los Angeles, he went only to Robinsons in Beverly Hills. Shirts were made for him by a special tailor in Spain or by a man called Tani in Tokyo with whom Grant had entered into negotiations many years before. Grant would order, over the phone, a selection of striped and coloured shirts. When they arrived, he tried each on, with loving concentration. If they were anything short of perfect, they went back to Japan for alteration, and Grant would phone Tani his fresh specifications: 'extend the collar tip by ⅛ inch' would be the kind of request that would necessitate a 10,000-mile return journey.

Cary Grant

When clothes returned from the cleaners, Grant liked them to be left folded on his bed so that he could put them away exactly as he liked them, in his cupboards, hanging on wishbone hangers. Only he knew exactly how to control these immense cupboards, since they were operated by electronic switches hidden under the carpet. Open, they were a vision of sartorial splendour, with row upon row of dark suits, dating back over several decades, and below them lines of highly polished custom-made shoes, one almost identical to the next. Weaver noted with envy that there was something about Grant that made his clothes stay in perfect shape. While on other people clothes developed stains, creases, and spots, Grant's remained impeccable. Even his shoes never seemed to acquire scuff marks or the signs of wear.

If there were outings to be made during the afternoon – perhaps to a preview in one of the Hollywood studios, or to visit any one of the lawyers engaged in his custody battles over Jennifer – Weaver would pray that it would be him at the wheel of the Rolls-Royce. Grant was a terrible driver. He was apt to criss-cross casually from lane to lane on the freeways, ignoring any stop signs, and simply turning off abruptly on a sudden short cut he thought he remembered, paying no attention at all to whatever might be happening behind him. On one trip to Malibu Market Grant absent-mindedly pressed his foot firmly down on the accelerator pedal rather than the brake as the car approached the immense plate-glass window of a grocery store. There was a crack like a gun shot and shattered glass sprayed into the air. In a flash Grant was out of the car and in the store, so embarrassed that he told the startled shop manager there had been a sonic boom.

Another day, he decided to visit Farmer's Market in Hollywood. While parking the Rolls, he crashed straight into the back bumper of a car in front. Since the owner wasn't there, Grant told Weaver to leave a note with his – Weaver's – name and address. Before the note could be written, however, the woman who owned the car appeared on the scene, gesticulating angrily when she saw the dent in her car. Grant turned on her the full force of his considerable charm, gave her his autograph, and left her swearing that she would

90

keep the broken fender for as long as she lived. Grant, Weaver often remarked, got away with murder – just by being Grant.

The solitude of this way of life, fallen into almost by accident after Dyan's departure, did much to encourage the eccentric in Grant. Matters that might otherwise have seemed totally insignificant assumed enormous and threatening proportions. Grant would berate Weaver, whom he treated with a mixture of paternal concern and schoolmasterly guidance, for drinking too much soda pop, or eating the wrong kind of food. (Soda pop, in particular, was hateful to him, and he was furious when one day he found some empty bottles in the dustbin.) Someone must have overheard the conversation, for a couple of days later there appeared in Harrison Carroll's gossip column in the *Herald Examiner*: 'What wealthy, masculine star daily counts the number of soft drinks in his refrigerator and raises a fuss if his secretary has one?'

He seemed consumed with curiosity about the relationship between parents and children – particularly between fathers and their children – and made Weaver repeat, again and again, details of his own relationship with his father. In these exchanges, Grant seemed to be seeking reassurance, however much he assumed the role of father confessor.

On other occasions, Grant displayed a puritanical approach to money, refusing, for instance, to have more than one brake on the Rolls mended when both threatened to go. He also instructed Weaver to split 100,000 dollars up into 10 accounts, each in a separate bank, so as to get the most return from all the special offers and bonuses available to new clients.

Grant could be lavish with money as well, handing out $200 tips to headwaiters and generous sums to totally unknown laundrymen or post boys, just as he could be extremely thoughtful about the needs of old friends, particularly when he could do something to help anonymously: when Clifford Odets, the director for whom he had made *None but the Lonely Heart* in 1944 was dying, Grant sent him $4,000 towards his many expenses.

After this, Grant, with too much time on his hands, and deeply unhappy about the rest of his life, developed a series of fads that grew even more eccentric with time. He read articles about cancer and then gave up eating anything cooked on charcoal, saying that it encouraged the disease. He refused to allow pets of any kind in the house, maintaining that they were carriers of viruses. He developed a hatred of house plants. He turned on anyone who took out a cigarette while in his company, criticizing them for endangering their health – on one uncomfortable occasion, Weaver overheard him lecture Jackie Onassis for her smoking, while refusing to find her a light. He decided that he didn't like women to wear boots, saying that it made their feet too hot, or men with long hair, which he declared would get caught in elevator doors. At one stage he took to having his slacks cleaned one day, wearing them the next, then returning them to the laundry complaining that they had been badly pressed. Because it was Grant, they did nothing. Some of these eccentricities amused but also alarmed Weaver, who sensed, when they verged on the fanatic, that they could easily one day get out of hand.

Nowhere, perhaps, was his truly peculiar form of stinginess more evident than in his attitude towards the house in Palm Springs which he had bought from Thelma Orloff, a Goldwyn chorus girl, at the beginning of his marriage to Betsy Drake. Perhaps because he associated it with happier times, and therefore couldn't bear to go back to it, he treated it much the same way as he had his home in Beverly Grove Drive – only with rather more serious consequences.

When Weaver first set eyes on the Palm Springs house it reminded him of Tara, the house in *Gone With the Wind*, after it was ransacked. It was derelict, crumbling, overgrown. The pleasant Spanish-style house, with its thick adobe walls, painted tiles, and wrought-iron gates, had a look of utter abandon. In the sitting room, the formerly elegant chairs and sofas has mouldered in the damp so that stuffing protruded through ragged holes. Taps were rusty and leaking. In the garden, grapefruit and dates had been allowed to fall to the ground and now rotted in brownish mounds around the foot of the trees, smelling heavy, sweet, and sickly.

Weaver, looking around him, realized that unless the house had an occupant it would collapse altogether. He persuaded Grant to allow him to recruit a tenant who, in return for free lodging, would reclaim the jungle from its state of wilderness and carry out basic repair jobs inside the house.

The first tenant, a Mrs Evelyn Milan, stayed for some years and kept total disintegration at bay. The second, Miss Anwina Lovendahl, was an artist. She barely had time to paint all the walls deep purple before Weaver was sent to Palm Springs to evict her. Then came a German lady called Vera DeWinter who gave notice when she discovered that, among her other tasks, she was also expected to paint the swimming pool. She was followed by a health food enthusiast, Peter Goebe, who preferred to spend his time lifting weights than developing his muscles on more mundane jobs like repairs. Finally Grant heard of a middle-aged couple who had been handling the 'maintenance' at one of the Palm Springs country clubs. The word 'maintenance' by this time was balm to his ears.

These last tenants gave the *coup de grâce* to the Grant house. They began by installing a great number of their relations, many of them apparent former flower-children of the sixties who used the brocade and embroidery fabric from the furniture to make into shoulder bags. Under the strain of so many people the plumbing, already frail, collapsed altogether. When Weaver arrived in Palm Springs to remonstrate, the woman tenant reluctantly agreed to turn her horde of relations out into the garden to do some work. That first day a wind blew up. While the woman was desultorily scratching a few leaves with a rake from under a tree a great gust dislodged an enormous branch above her head, felling her to the ground. The hospital where she was taken reported several bones broken, severe internal bleeding, and temporary blindness. She promptly sued Grant, and won.

In the early days when no one ever came to visit Grant at home, Weaver put it down to reluctance on Grant's part to allow friends to see the shabbiness of Beverly Grove Drive. Later, when the house was patched up and more or less redecorated, and still no one came, he understood that this was all part of Grant's genuine misanthropy, severely aggravated by the collapse of his marriage. Grant didn't want people. He preferred to be alone. In the ten years that Weaver worked for him, Grant hardly ever invited anyone for a meal or for company.

Grant also loathed going out. A natural tendency towards solitary domesticity, present all his life, and even during his four marriages – all four wives bitterly complained about it – was increased many times over in the late 1960s and early 1970s, while Grant grappled to come to terms with being alone again, and with having lost his only child. He was, Weaver observed, enormously shy – and during these unhappy years after Dyan's departure, neurotically so – and would work himself into a state of anguish and torment when any event of a challenging nature was suggested.

Whenever he could, Grant attended only the smallest of gatherings, with only the closest of friends. Just occasionally, however, he would be trapped into larger engagements – formal ceremonials of the cinema world, for instance. At these times, Weaver would seriously fear for him.

Early in 1970, when Dyan had been gone barely three years, and the Beverly Grove Drive house was in one of its periodic bouts of redecoration, Grant was asked by Alexander Cohen, producer of the Antoine Perry Award Show, to present an honorary 'Tony' to Noel Coward. Coward was an old friend of Grant's, from Broadway days when Coward was the toast of the town and Archibald Leach a beginner trying out his luck on the boards. For the sake of old times, Grant could scarcely refuse.

As the date of the occasion grew nearer, he worked himself up into an unhappy and restless mood of constant fretfulness. One of his more acute worries was that he would perspire so much in his terror of the crowd and the demands put on him that the sweat would begin to show through his dinner jacket. He finally came up with a solution, and asked Weaver to find him some pads to sew into the jacket sleeves.

Katharine Hepburn and Lauren Bacall, two good friends of

Grant, were contenders that night for the Best Actress award. When Grant and Weaver reached the New York theatre where the presentation was taking place, they found the backstage area full of friends and very merry. Shirley Maclaine, Alfred Lunt, Lynn Fontanne, and Maggie Smith were all milling around talking. The informality of their mood soon conveyed itself to Grant who began at last to calm down.

Grant, however, seemed doomed to scenes of comic confusion worthy of a Marx Brothers' movie. In the flurry of the evening, no one thought to explain either to him or to Weaver, who kept by him like a shadow, just where Grant was supposed to make his entrance. All they knew was that, while Noel Coward was to reach the stage down a glittering staircase from above, Grant was to meet him coming up from below out of the bowels of the theatre. Split-second timing was clearly crucial.

The auditorium set aside for the evening was the Mark Hellinger Theater where Katharine Hepburn was currently appearing in *Coco*. The sets were immense and extraordinarily elaborate; vast mechanical monsters cluttered the backstage, reflected a hundred times over in the huge mirrored staircases used during *Coco* for scenes of Chanel fashion shows. When Grant and Weaver set off through them to make their way to rendezvous with Coward, they discovered that they had no idea about how to get there, and so wandered, in growing agitation, among the hydraulic equipment, seeing their own reflections magnified and repeated in the great mirrors, as if in a futuristic maze leading to nowhere. At last Grant caught sight of a light coming from a distant corner. He sped off towards it, scrambling over wires and round machinery, with Weaver panting along behind him, and burst out onto the stage at the precise moment that Coward began his stately descent down the triumphal staircase. There was resounding applause. The muddle, however, had not been guaranteed to soothe Grant's nerves.

After the presentation was over, the police formed themselves into a human barricade outside the theatre to hold back the vast mob crowding the street from crushing the stars to death as they stepped into their limousines. The Awards were one way of honouring the performers; the public had its own way, rather more cruel and very much more noisy. As each star emerged from the theatre door, they were greeted by varying amounts of acclaim, from the merely polite clapping to the boisterous ovation.

Shirley Maclaine appeared, smiled, and was clapped, in a friendly but subdued way. James Stewart drew appreciative and steady applause. The Lunts were greeted with affection and respect. Maggie Smith was cheered.

But then Grant stepped through the door. In a second the police barricade was scattered as fans, young, middle-aged, and old, erupted through the cordon, rushing to try to touch the man they still regarded as their idol, clutching out at him, shoving, pushing, and kicking, tearing at his buttons in order to secure at least one small trophy of the star. Grant was jostled and shoved. A small gold comb was torn from his back pocket.

The experience was overwhelming, and extremely heartening for a star who had not appeared in a movie for over four years. But it was not a particularly pleasant one, and Grant, already in a fragile and uncertain frame of mind, could be forgiven for wishing only to retreat back up to his mountain eyrie and remain there, undisturbed, for ever.

7

Making Millions

What Bill Weaver could never have guessed when he went to work for Grant at Universal in the mid-1960s was that he had arrived just in time to witness the actor's final appearance on screen. *Walk, Don't Run* was not a box-office success – perhaps because for once Grant didn't want the girl. Grant himself was extremely conscious of the difficulties of a screen metamorphosis into old age. After *Father Goose* some years before he had announced, 'I'm too old for that stuff. The kids don't like to see me playing bedroom scenes with young leading ladies.' Now, with bad reviews and bad returns, he became convinced that the public only really wanted to see him as a romantic figure. Age had put an end to that.

Offers, however, continued to pour in, and Grant treated them, as he treated the reporters who came to ask him why he wasn't making any more movies, with his customary charm and civility. When offered a part in *Sleuth*, he announced that 'it would be too much work. I mean I've *done* all that – almost seventy times. And it's a tiresome and very strenuous business.' When Jack Warner selected him to play the mellifluous Professor Higgins in *My Fair Lady*, he turned that down too, saying that 'once something has been done to perfection, why interfere with success?' And then he joked: 'I guess you can say that I'm retired from the movies until some writer comes up with a character who is deaf and dumb and sitting in a wheelchair.'

This was Grant, coping with importunate questions with his familiar ease. But, Weaver soon came to understand, the actual

97

reason behind Grant's decision to leave the world of the movies was far more simple than a desire not to age on screen. Grant didn't want to make movies any more. He was tired of the whole business. As he pointed out to his secretary, he was fast reaching the age when any other professional man would be thinking of retiring. 'Don't grave-diggers retire at sixty-five?' he would ask Weaver. 'And what about executives?' He was through with films, with the exhausting hours, the dirt, the confusion, the pressures, and the hard work. Since he didn't actually need to make more films, why on earth should he?

And then there was Jennifer to consider. Her birth had coincided neatly with the end of *Walk, Don't Run*, thereby providing him with an excellent excuse to stop work and spend more time with his only child. How much more convenient, once Dyan had left him, not to take up that punishing routine again, but be available instead to spend what time he was allowed enjoying the child to the full. And so the years of Jennifer's infancy passed, and Grant was able to say: 'I seldom go to the movies. I realize that they fill an enormous gap for many people. But not for me. I am more attracted to the world of reality.'

Reality, for Grant, was not, as some friends began to suspect, idleness. On the contrary, never had Grant been so active as during the years following his departure from the studios. It was a very different sort of activity from anything he had been used to, but one that anyone who knew anything about Grant's past would have been quick to realize was exactly right for him: he became a businessman. He joined the boards of companies, and tried his hand at public relations, and he took to managing his own affairs to a large extent. This was a new world for him, and he was to prove himself excellent at it: Cary Grant the businessman was just as capable, just as successful – in all the ways that the word entails – as Cary Grant the film star.

When people came to ask themselves just what Grant was now getting up to, they remembered his reputation as the first Hollywood star to escape the exclusive studio contract and also the first to negotiate a ten per cent cut of the gross deal (not to mention one of the first to use a lawyer on a fixed salary, rather than an agent, taking ten per cent, to negotiate his contracts.) Even so, that wasn't going back far enough. Grant was also one of the first Broadway artists in the late 1920s to resist a long-term contract with a theatrical entrepreneur – normally the most prized of arrangements for its security – in favour of independence.

In fact, anyone choosing to examine Grant's past, when it came to financial arrangements, would have detected in the deals the presence of a shrewd and canny business mind. And these deals were not just cleverly thought out; they were also full of foresight.

For one thing, the decision he took in 1936 never to sign on again with a studio on an exclusive basis meant that, unlike every other film star right up until the 1950s, Grant was able to pick his own scripts and select the directors he particularly liked working with. He was able, in fact, to mould his own screen persona in a way that other stars, like Gary Cooper, beholden to the big studios, could not. More than anyone, Cary Grant shaped Cary Grant, fashioned the charming, wry, self-deprecating hero of romantic comedies, picking his way delicately through misunderstandings and narrow escapes.

It also meant money, for within a short time of leaving Paramount he was in a position to command $150,000 for every film – and that was only the beginning. Later he set up partnerships and became a producer of his own films through his own corporations, which bore names like Granley, Granox, and Granart – combinations of Grant's name and his attorney's, Stanley Fox.

Nor did his business acumen stop at the deals. To make certain that his films played in the Radio City Music Hall in New York – and twenty-eight did – he would personally have the film screened for potential exhibitors in a large theatre so that his audience would get the feel of how large numbers of people would react to the film. 'If your pictures make the Music Hall,' he would explain, 'you don't have to persuade smaller theatres to take it.'

But that, from a financial point of view, was just the start of it. When Grant realized that eventually his films would be bound to be sold for television, he announced that he would no longer star in any film unless he acquired ownership of the negative, seven years after the film was released. By now he had his full-time financial assistant to handle the negotiations: the ex-naval captain and attorney Stanley Fox, who had joined Grant in the 1940s on a fixed salary to handle all his deals. (Over the many years of their association, the two men came to look extraordinarily alike: tall, thin, distinguished, greying elegantly.)

This was another shrewd move. In the early 1970s National Telefilm Associates paid Grant over $2 million for his equity in seven films – among them *Indiscreet* with Ingrid Bergman, *Operation Petticoat* with Tony Curtis, and *That Touch of Mink* with Doris Day. If this calculated approach to movie making seems to detract somewhat from the utterly unvenal Cary Grant screen figure, it is only because stars aren't meant to be financiers as well. But as Grant himself once said to a reporter: 'I was never interested in films: I was interested in the economics of the business. . .' He was pulling his leg, of course, but not entirely.

Not long after Grant left his bungalow at Universal and departed for the hills as a private citizen, he was invited by George Barrie, president of Fabergé, the cosmetics company, to join their board of directors. Barrie was an acquaintance of Grant, a slight, energetic, flamboyant figure with very curly salt-and-pepper hair. He was immensely wealthy, with a farm in Connecticut and an apartment in the United Nations Plaza Apartments in New York, of which Truman Capote was another tenant. Barrie had also been a saxophone player in his youth, and he and Grant would occasionally play together, with Grant at the organ or the piano. They weren't close, but they were friends.

It wasn't specifically spelt out, but the understanding behind Barrie's offer was that this polished idol of the American screen, possibly better known and loved than any other living actor, would make a fetching public relations symbol for the company. And so it turned out.

Grant, ever energetic and extremely conscientious about his working commitments, threw himself into his role with surprising

100

relish – surprising in that it demanded of him precisely the undertakings that, elsewhere in his life, he was so assiduously avoiding. To fulfil his role, he had to be seen by the public, he had to appear at presentations, he had to give away awards, and he had to make speeches. None of these were things that Grant cared to do. Yet, paradoxically, perhaps precisely because it was work and therefore simply another branch of acting, he didn't seem to mind.

Grant's specific task consisted of attending a board meeting every three months. More nebulously, he built into his way of life strategies for promoting Fabergé products. When he was visiting a city he would contact the biggest store carrying Fabergé products and tell them that he would drop by at a certain hour; the PR department would then arrange for news coverage so that Grant would be captured by photographers as he leaned, grinning, across a counter laden with scent.

'Come to Dallas' one store was able to advertise. 'We guarantee you $1 million in sales in one day.' The draw of Cary Grant's physical presence seemed to know no bounds: on one occasion, the buyers from two major West Coast shops abruptly changed their schedules because he came to town to take them and their wives to Las Vegas for dinner. On another, only the rumour that Grant would be appearing at one store's charity show tripled the management's usual take for its favourite fund.

For the public, Cary Grant off screen was as appealing as he had been on it, as funny, as apparently prone to near disasters, above all as elegant and charming. As he became more practised at it, so he perfected a seemingly chaotic manner at presentations which was in fact nothing other than the slickest of routines. He would fumble with his introductions, drop his glasses, grope around on the floor for them. He also became a master of the instant joke. Not long after Grant joined them, Fabergé introduced awards for summer stock actors and actresses called the Straw Hat Awards. Usually it fell to Grant to act as compère. 'It has been said,' he declared on one occasion, as he stood to give the prizes, 'that Helen Gallagher was born dancing.' Then he paused, an old hand at timing. 'Rough on her mother wasn't it?'

101

With time, Grant even perfected a line for journalists. To each one who came to ask him how he could bear to swap the movie studios for peddling cosmetics, Grant would patiently explain that his new role was in many ways precisely like his old one, in that he had always 'merchandised' his own films. 'The same kind of merchandising works for the fragrance business,' he would say. 'If you sell to the large department stores – as I sold my films to Radio City Music Hall – then the smaller ones fall in.'

He would go on: 'Co-operative advertising is also the same for films as it is for fragrances. Theatre and movie companies often share the price of advertising. We also share advertising costs with the department stores we do business with.

'Then there is the researching to consider. We researched Fabergé's Brut just as you would research a screen-play. Then we ask ourselves where the raw essence can be found (which would be like finding a location for a movie) and how to get the quantities (the prints) in case we've got a hit.'

And he would finish: 'Perfumes are dramatic. . . In this business of course my reviews come out of the shopping columns. . .' It was all very plausible and the reporters wrote it all down.

Of course, there were the perks. Grant didn't actually need them – his business deals had ensured that he was already an immensely rich man – but they came on a scale and with a splendour that not even the richest of men could actually shrug off. Grant, understandably, loved them.

There was, first of all, the salary, which ran to some $25,000 a year as a director of the board. But this was the least of it. Fabergé, under George Barrie, had a stable of private planes and helicopters freely put to Grant's use so that a trip from Los Angeles to New York might consist of a private jet to Newark, New Jersey, and two helicopters for the last leg in to the top of the Pan Am Building on Park Avenue, one for Grant and Weaver and one for the luggage.

In time, however, Grant was given a plane of his own. When asked what kind he would like, he stated that he didn't want a jet at any price, because he intended to travel slowly, without frenzy. Fabergé came up with a 1930s DC3, a dignified old-fashioned

102

aircraft, like something out of his early movies, with a tail that dipped to the ground.

Part of the deal was that Grant should be allowed to redecorate the plane, now in a somewhat dilapidated state. Showing none of his customary prevarication, he had it done up rather like a small bungalow, with an ash dining table and four chocolate-brown swivelling chairs, a collection of bright yellow armchairs (with antimacassars from Spain, a present from Rose Wells, head buyer for all the federated stores in the country), and two sofas, in tomato red and green. Along one side of the plane was a lazy Susan bar: at the press of a button, a contraption bearing bottles would rise up from the heart of the plane; on the other stood a piano, fastened down to the floor, at which Grant would sit playing his usual medley of songs during long journeys across the country. The windows – huge picture windows giving a panoramic view of the sky – were hung with his invariable canvas curtains, once again in white, with green tassels. There was a galley and a bathroom, and the walls of the plane were covered with photographs of Jennifer. The atmosphere was one of cosy domesticity and cheerfulness – in marked contrast, as Grant would point out, to the usual furnishings of modern aircraft – and he and Weaver sometimes slept the night on board to avoid publicity on overnight stops between the East and West Coasts. He liked the fact that there were no telephones nor other means of disturbance. Weaver, who brought his typewriter along with him, worked.

Not all the journeys on board the DC3 were business trips. As Grant got into the swing of this new toy, he would use it to fly to Catalina Island with Jennifer for lunch, or to San Francisco for dinner at a celebrated Chinese restaurant owned by Johnny Kan, author of a cookbook of Chinese recipes, a man he greatly admired. After dinner, Grant would go down into the kitchens, call for the chef, and ask to be taught the recipe of what he had just eaten.

It was on the Fabergé plane that Grant made a sad pilgrimage of farewell to his former stepson, Lance Reventlow. He had been fond of the boy during the years of his marriage to Barbara Hutton, and had taken pains to keep up with him after they were separated.

103

Though temperamentally very different – Lance went through a rich playboy phase, driving fast racing cars – they continued to meet all through Lance's brief marriage to the actress Jill St John, and still later, when Lance had married a former Disney 'mouseketeer' called Cheryl Haldridge and bought himself a house in Aspen, Colorado.

In the summer of 1972, Lance boarded a single-engine plane with a surveyor to look at some property that he was thinking of buying. He never returned. The plane ran into a thunderstorm, was sucked into a downcurrent, and crashed. The bodies of all four passengers were burned beyond recognition.

Barbara Hutton wanted the remains of her only child to be interred in the Woolworth crypt in New York, and was most upset when Cheryl insisted on respecting Lance's own wish that his ashes be scattered in the mountains round Aspen that he loved so much. Braving Barbara Hutton's displeasure, Grant, Jill St John, who lived across the valley from him, and Weaver flew down to Colorado in the DC3. Aspen's small orchestra had agreed to perform a requiem mass in an open-air pavilion. Grant joined the mourners as they walked from the house to the pavilion, led by Cheryl, who was barefoot. After the mass, somewhat to his discomfort, there was a loud rock concert, blared out over stereophonic speakers.

Later, flying home, Jill St John told Grant that three months earlier she had been to see a medium in Los Angeles who had forecast Lance's death, exactly as it had happened. Barbara Hutton couldn't bring herself to accept what had happened: she never got in touch with Grant again.

Much of Grant's Fabergé business took place in New York, where the company had offices on the Avenue of the Americas. To house him while in town, George Barrie found him a penthouse at the Warwick Hotel, a few minutes' walk away, which had been bought, decades before, by Randolph Hearst as a gift for Marion Davies. The apartment retained all the former 1930s glory, including the wooden beams, transported from San Simeon, as well as ornate mirrors and mouldings. For Grant, the Warwick penthouse had the added pleasure of belonging to a triumphant period of his earlier life. Not long after arriving in Hollywood, at the height of his first glory in the movie business, Grant had been befriended by the Hearst family and spent many enjoyable evenings in their rather extravagant company. These outings had been brought to an abrupt close after Grant and Randolph Hearst Junior had taken a small plane up one day and flown low over the turrets and crenellations of San Simeon, dropping bags of white flour in a simulated bombing of the estate. These highjinks, so beloved of Grant and so much part of the more sunny side of his character on screen as well as off it, were not of the kind to amuse the newspaper magnate.

The penthouse also possessed a magnificent terrace on which Grant could continue with his ritual sunbathing – but only at weekends. He learned his lesson about the other days early on in the occupancy of the penthouse. On the first fine morning after he had moved in, Grant fetched a deck-chair and stretched himself out in the sun, as always in his swimming trunks. Within minutes, there was a cacophony of tapping, as if an army of woodpeckers had been released in a forest. It was the secretaries who worked in the skyscraper that overlooked the Warwick. When Grant, jolted out of a drowsy reverie, looked up, he saw that every window for many floors up contained women rapping rhythmically on the glass to attract his attention. What made the spectacle all the more amazing was the fact that not one tapper seemed conscious of any of the others, but believed herself alone in signalling to the movie star. Only from Grant's position could the full absurdity of the scene be understood. 'A chorus of crickets' was how he described the event later, adding that it had been 'flattering but frustrating'. After that he stayed indoors on weekdays.

Fabergé offered to have the apartment redecorated, for by now much of the furniture was threadbare, but here Grant's dilatoriness returned. He did engage an interior decorator, but soon lost interest in his plans, and the apartment stayed as it was. Perhaps once a month Grant and Weaver would pack their bags and travel across America for a couple of nights at the Warwick, where Grant would complain that the bacon was no longer edible after its twenty-seven-floor journey up from the hotel kitchens, and send Weaver out for endless breakfasts from a delicatessen on Sixth Avenue. The rest of the time the penthouse stood empty.

Yet it was at the Warwick that Grant had many enjoyable reunions with East Coast friends, who would come up to the penthouse to visit him and drink scotch out of his monogrammed glasses, a much-prized gift from one of his fans. One of these was William McIntosh, who came to visit Grant one day with the suggestion that he star in a film to be called *Kotch* about to be produced by JALEM, Jack Lemmon's production company. Grant glanced at the script, the story of an older man and a young girl, both tossed out of their families and seeking to make a life on their own, and declined, saying: 'I'm not going to trip over any damned sound cords again. I've tripped over far too many in my time.' (Walter Matthau took the part instead.)

On another occasion, when McIntosh had come to discuss another business venture, the electric power at the Warwick failed. McIntosh was due to meet Jack Lemmon and his wife Felicia at the Sherry Netherlands Hotel for a drink. After waiting in the hope that the power would return he finally decided to walk the twenty-seven flights down to the ground floor, despite the intense summer heat. When he left, he carried in his hand a beaker of whisky, in one of Grant's beloved monogrammed glasses, to smooth the journey down. In due course, a packet arrived for Grant. It was a set of identical monogrammed glasses, a present from McIntosh. Grant immediately despatched one of his funny and impetuous letters of thanks, more script, with its staccato sentences and rhetorical questions, than formal letter, full of affection and pleasure.

There was another perk too, alongside the plane and the hotel suite and the cars and the endlessly paid bills: Weaver's salary. On the one hand, the fact that Fabergé was going to pay him spelt security for Weaver – Grant had long treated the subject of Weaver's salary with a sort of paternalistic nonchalance, never exactly generous – but on the other, it was a chancy step to take. George Barrie, in making the offer, had explained to the secretary: 'What we do in this company is to pay our people whatever they think they're worth, and if it then turns out that they're not worth it, we fire them.' (The salary turned out to be considerably larger than the one Weaver had been receiving directly from Grant.)

Perks aside, there was no question that Grant earned his salary. He was endlessly attending events and opening galas on behalf of the company. Apart from all his unspecified work as public relations man, there was his involvement with Brut Productions, a film company set up by George Barrie in which Grant's expertise proved invaluable. (Invaluable, he insisted, not essential; to reporters who flocked to ask him whether the whole thing had been his idea in the first place, he firmly reported that it was all Barrie's idea.)

Brut Productions was launched well. The company brought out *Night Watch* with Elizabeth Taylor, and *A Touch of Class* with Glenda Jackson and George Segal, which cost $2 million to make and grossed $3.5 million during its first four weeks, as well as winning four Academy Award nominations and an Oscar for Glenda Jackson. George Barrie, in memory of his saxophone-playing days, composed the title song. Grant, to everyone who hinted that this must surely be his way back into the movies, would only say that he was the film's press agent and that was all. 'I have,' he said, 'no notion of getting back into pictures nor do I have the strength.'

After Brut Productions, came a number of trips abroad for the company, usually made together with George Barrie and other directors. There was one to Czechoslovakia for a trade fair and another to Japan on a promotion tour. These, for Grant, were a mixed success. He played his part with distinction and was invariably much fêted by his hosts – Weaver, in particular, found the trip to Tokyo immensely pleasurable in that he didn't have to fear for Grant's well-being in the midst of the orderly Japanese crowds – but increasingly he felt distanced from his fellow Fabergé directors. There was something about Barrie, with his ebullience, his jokes, his flamboyance, that jarred with Grant's own more subtle and restrained style. Grant didn't enjoy staying up late; he wasn't a great drinker, nor did he like dirty jokes. There was something in these junkets that depressed him.

In time, Grant's involvement with Fabergé grew a little more distant. A feeling in the company that Barrie was somewhat over-generous with his perks brought the private plane arrangement – by now the DC3 had been replaced by a Convair – to an end, though Grant continued to have use of the company's jets. (Grant's plane, in use no more than a few times a month, had kept two pilots on permanent standby.) He remained an active member of the board, but a more cautious one, and, Weaver felt, was increasingly wary of being used too commercially. Business, he seemed to have decided, was immensely enjoyable, but it had to be treated with circumspection.

The Las Vegas Strip in Nevada, paradise for the world's gamblers, is made up of long blocks of hotels and casinos. By day the Strip is shoddy, a little depressing. But at night, as darkness falls across the desert, a million neon lights miraculously transform it into a land of glamour and dreams. Inside the casinos, however, that moment of sudden illumination passes unnoticed: there, night and day are as one, with no clocks visible to remind the gamblers of the passing hours and one long round of free drinks to keep their spirits up. It is all very gaudy and colourful and, for the winners, very exciting.

Las Vegas casino life appears an extremely improbable setting for Cary Grant. There would seem to be in his character too much fastidiousness, too much attention to style, for him to be able to find pleasure amid such vulgarity. And yet Las Vegas was important to him. It involved his past, his early days in America, his first friends; they were commitments and bonds he never chose to sever – indeed, he selected Las Vegas as the city in which to marry Dyan Cannon. To understand something of this attachment, one has to go back to the birth of Las Vegas itself.

The Strip was the brainchild of a New York mobster called Benjamin 'Bugsy' Siegel who travelled west shortly after the war to escape his gangland past, heading for Nevada, which, in an attempt to survive the Depression of the early 1930s, had legalized gambling. He decided to ignore Reno, in the north, because that already had casinos. Instead, he settled his dreams on a small parcel of land just outside the city limits of Las Vegas – itself no more than a couple of gas stations providing travellers across the Nevada desert with the means of keeping on the move – called Las Vegas Boulevard South, or, more colloquially, the Strip.

Reviving ancient gambling contacts, Siegel collected $1 million towards the construction of a hotel casino he intended to name the Fabulous Flamingo. Foundations began to rise alongside the edge of the desert. But then costs escalated, progress on the casino slowed down, and Siegel's Mafia friends were on the point of ordering him 'hit' when he managed to set an opening date – 26 December 1946 – and thus won a reprieve.

It was short lived. The opening night was a disaster. No one, it turned out, wanted to spend their Christmas holidays in the centre of an unknown desert in the middle of Nevada. The Mafia reclaimed the hotel and opened it again themselves in May 1947. But by then Siegel was dead, blasted to pieces by a shotgun while staying with his girlfriend in Los Angeles.

The sad thing for Siegel was that he had been right about Las Vegas. The Flamingo was so enormously successful that soon other hotel casinos rose up all around it on the Strip, many, though not all, controlled by the Mafia.

In November 1966 Howard Hughes came to Las Vegas. He had been there before, of course, but as a visitor, dressed in a crumpled suit and canvas shoes, gambling at the craps table. Now he was coming to settle, already a recluse, his affairs in the hands of a former F.B.I. man called Bob Maheu, and all his communications with the outside world made through five Mormon male personal aides. Hughes was seeking privacy, anonymity – and a stake in the great wealth of the casinos.

He may have been one of America's richest men, but Hughes was not a desirable customer. He was, as the hotel casino managers well knew, looking for long-term accommodation, not gambling; and in Las Vegas it is the gamblers who provide the profit.

Maheu first approached a hotel called the Dunes owned by Charlie Rich, but there the management would only release half a floor. Next he tried Wilbur Clark's Desert Inn, securing for Hughes the use of the entire ninth floor, consisting of seven penthouse suites. At first there was no trouble, but as the weeks passed and Hughes and his entourage showed no signs of moving on – the casino reckoned that they were losing them $3,000 a day – pressure began to build up. Hughes solved it in his customary way. He simply bought the hotel, or at least a lease to operate its casino, for $13 million. Then he went on to buy others. Not everywhere was he greeted with wholehearted pleasure. When he took over the Sands, considered to be the pride of the Strip, renting its 777 rooms at $100 a day each, Frank Sinatra, who performed there regularly and felt proprietary about it, told an audience: 'You're wondering why I don't have a drink in my hand. Howard Hughes bought it.'

After the Sands, came the Castaways, with 230 cheap rooms, bawdy revues and low-stake gambling, and the Silver Slipper. Then came the day when Hughes, through Maheu, announced that he would be putting up the 'New Sands', the 'most complete vacation and pleasure complex anywhere in the world'. The New Sands was nothing but a dream and it was never built; the point of it was that Hughes, in mid-expansion, had suddenly become anxious about competition.

The main threat to his empire, as he saw it, came from a man called Kirk Kerkorian, a dark, quiet-spoken Armenian, who had his hair in a quiff and wore Italian silk suits and alligator shoes, and who had made his fortune in the airline business. Kerkorian, like Hughes, was a pilot, and he had spent the war instructing U.S. pilots and ferrying planes to England for the Royal Air Force.

In 1947, he started a charter airline, Los Angeles Air Service, which in time became Trans International Airlines, sold by Kerkorian in 1967 for $90 million worth of stock in Transamerican Corporation.

Kerkorian, like Hughes, believed that there was money to be made on the Strip. In the late 1960s he became landlord of Caesar's Palace, and he was able to outbid Hughes for the Fabulous Flamingo, reopening it with a splurge of extravagance and panache by having the wife of one of the hotel dignitaries lifted ninety feet into the air on an electronic boom in order to pour champagne over the beak of a flamingo made of neon, which, with the assistance of a computer, two miles of fluorescent tubing, and 6,000 bulbs, fluttered its pink feathers.

That didn't bother Hughes. What did was Kerkorian's stated intention of building a new hotel-casino, to be called the International, 'the biggest and costliest gambling complex of its kind in Las Vegas'. What was more, no sooner had the scheme been announced, than work on it began.

On the other side of Paradise Road, opposite the site of the International, stood a thirty-one-storey building called the Landmark Tower, empty since its completion in 1966 because of law suits. Hughes now put in a bid for the hotel, offering to pay off the various creditors as well as parting with a sum of $17 million. Once again through Maheu, he announced that the New Landmark would open, with an enormous jamboree, on 1 July 1969. Immediately, Kerkorian retaliated with an announcement of his own. The International, he declared, would open with an equally flamboyant celebration on 2 July.

These men, improbably, were Grant's friends. They were men he knew well, and had known for a long time, and as their fortunes had become inextricably linked with Las Vegas and the gamblers, so, inevitably, had Grant come along for the ride. He knew Howard Hughes from the days when he had owned the RKO Studios, and the two men had shared dates (Hughes was best man at his marriage to Betsy Drake). He knew Charlie Rich from the times when they went to boxing matches together, sat in the front row, and were splattered by blood from the boxers (Rich was best man at his marriage to Dyan Cannon, and Grant sometimes went to spend weekends with him in his Palm Springs house). He knew Kerkorian from Los Angeles – and was now on the board of Western Airlines,

111

Kerkorian's regional carrier. He knew Frank Sinatra from the days when both had starred with Sophia Loren in Spain in *The Pride and the Passion* (and he had been with Sinatra to take his mother out on Mother's Day to a New York restaurant called Jilly's, owned by the crooner's bodyguard and much frequented by him). He had even known Bugsy Siegel, through his old friend Dorothy di Frasso, the cosmopolitan countess who introduced him to Barbara Hutton. And because these men were friends he was willing to do things for them, to help them to promote their hotels and their casinos, even if he was no gambler himself and the flavour of the place seemed, on the face of it, very alien to his nature. There was about these entrepreneurs something that attracted Grant, just as in Los Angeles he spent some time with Bernie Cornfeld, the IOS financier – something that he found easier to handle than the more touchy, brittle world of Hollywood.

In return, of course, there were bonuses. The Dunes, Charlie Rich's hotel, had a Cary Grant suite reserved entirely for him, never used when he wasn't there. It was enough to have Grant strolling through the lobbies among the gamblers to confer a touch of stardom and respectability on the place and the hotel managers knew precisely how to make the most of it, seating Grant where he would be most often picked up by the cameras. Grant, in this context, and like any other celebrity, was bait. Later, other hotels and complexes followed suit. The MGM Grand set aside a Cary Grant room, as it did for a number of its former Hollywood stars.

There was, too, about the whole Las Vegas world, incredible luxury. Things were done, if not exactly in style, then at least at considerable expense, so that outings took on all the trappings of full-blown Hollywood productions. As a director of the board of Western Airlines, Grant quite often flew on Kirk Kerkorian's DC9, a plane decked out to resemble a hotel-cum-office, with beds for eight people, two bathrooms with showers, an office section with electric typewriters and telephones, and the latest in television sets and cassette recorders. Gourmet food, worthy of a starred restaurant, was served en route.

In the summer of 1969 Grant and Weaver flew down to Las

Vegas for Hughes' grand opening of the Landmark. It was indeed an extraordinary occasion, with the outside glass elevator crawling up and down the west wing of the space-age, needle-shaped hotel, as celebrities in evening dress crowded to see a panoramic, thirty-one-storey high, view of the Strip stretched below them. 'The scene,' commented a newspaper next morning, 'resembled a Hollywood première.'

(Grant, who had always admired Hughes greatly – it was the recluse's desire for austerity that inspired Grant, Weaver suspected, to live as frugally and simply as possible, and with as few material possessions – did not meet his friend. In fact, he never saw him again. Some years later, in the early 1970s, he happened to be staying at the Inn on the Park in London when Hughes alighted there briefly, but knowing his hatred of all intrusion, and the fact that he was by now a very sick man, Grant made no attempt to contact him. He did, however, make one gesture of salute to his former flying friend. As Grant and Weaver got out of the lift on Hughes' floor, Grant raised his hand towards a television camera positioned outside Hughes' suite, and gave a wave, suspecting that Hughes himself might well be monitoring the cameras. It was a last farewell to an ageing, sick, and now very paranoid hero.)

In 1973, Grant was back in Las Vegas for another opening. This was for the new $106 million MGM Grand Hotel, which promised a month-long gala opening, starting with a Who's Who of Hollywood's 'golden era' in which stars of the past were ferried to the front of the Grand in vintage cars. Grant, who was to preside over a number of the festivities was by now also on the board of MGM, having been invited to join it by Kirk Kerkorian, who now owned the studio.

Grant had invited Raquel Welch and William McIntosh to accompany him to Las Vegas for the opening aboard Kerkorian's DC9. The party of Grant, Welch, McIntosh, and Weaver reached the city in the afternoon and found the Strip in a state of considerable excitement. (Las Vegas was always a headache for Weaver: it was the one place where he insisted on having bodyguards for Grant provided by the hotel, feeling incapable on his own of shielding his employer from the rapacious, predatory hands of the crowds who thronged the casino lobbies.) They checked into the Grand where they found a suite each waiting for them, consisting of a sitting room, two bedrooms, a bathroom, and a well-stocked bar, done up in gaudy colours, plush, frills, and French reproduction furniture. (But it was an ordeal reaching their rooms, with onlookers in the lobby jostling Raquel Welch and Grant, pulling at their clothes and clamouring for autographs.)

At dinner, Grant found himself at a table with a former mistress of Bugsy Siegel, now an elderly lady covered in diamonds wearing a bright-red satin, strapless ballgown. She had a permanent suite at the Sahara, having been left enough money in Siegel's will to see out her lifetime. William McIntosh was there, and so were Kirk Kerkorian and his wife, Kerkorian wearing a solid gold watch encrusted with diamonds.

Later that night, Raquel Welch suddenly decided that she needed to get back to Los Angeles. She was starting work on a new film next day and was needed at the studios by eight. Grant, plainly irritated by this last-minute change of plans, asked Weaver and McIntosh whether they would be kind enough to pack up Raquel Welch's suite for a speedy departure. The flight back to Los Angeles passed in stony silence. Grant, who didn't care for a disruption in his arrangements, and was in any case annoyed by Raquel Welch's self-centredness, distanced himself from the whole party.

That Las Vegas was part of his life and widely recognized to be so was plain from the fact that when Lord Louis Mountbatten, Prince Philip's uncle, was to pay a visit to the city on the way back from a tour of the Far East, it was Grant who was asked to accompany him. Grant, who had met Mountbatten before and greatly admired him, had accepted. But when the day arrived, a fresh court battle over Jennifer's custody was in full swing in Los Angeles and he simply refused to go. Weaver was despatched instead. This sudden cancellation was not calculated to please. Weaver had the discomforting experience of travelling most of the way from New York to Las Vegas on the Fabergé private jet that had been set aside for Mountbatten's use, in total silence, having been informed that protocol demanded that no one speak to his lordship unless he himself indicated that he wished for conversation. It was not until the plane was approaching Nevada that Weaver was called to Mountbatten's side and asked where the devil Grant had got to. (Weaver witnessed one of Mountbatten's idiosyncratic habits: throughout the journey he sat reading the newspaper, and each time he finished a page he simply tore it out and hurled it over his shoulder in to the aisle, whereupon a member of his entourage, who appeared to have no other role, leapt to his feet and retrieved it.)

Few of Grant's other friends ever understood the Las Vegas side to his character. They couldn't work out what he had in common with these most unlikely of companions, whose very way of behaviour seemed so utterly unlike his own. Nor could they see why he seemed to prefer the tawdriness and tinsel of the casinos to the more sedate and desirable exclusiveness of Palm Springs. But that Grant liked the Las Vegas world, and seemed to need it, was beyond doubt.

8

Leading Ladies

One day in the early 1970s, Cary Grant was asked by a reporter why he had chosen to become an actor. He thought for a while, then said: 'I probably chose my profession because I was seeking adulation, admiration, and affection, each a degree of love. Perhaps no child ever feels the recipient of enough love. Oh, how secretly we yearn for it, yet openly defend against it.'

The anxious need for affection, the striving to please, so as to be loved, seems to have been an important ingredient in Grant's apparently Jekyll and Hyde personality. It was sometimes as if he couldn't ever get quite enough of it, so that he had to keep looking for more, and yet when he got it, he felt the compulsion to destroy all that he had won. As the years went by, particularly after his experiments with LSD had unleashed a confessional vein in him (as witnessed by his article for the *Ladies' Home Journal*), he took to producing a little-boy-lost attitude towards people who questioned him about his marriages. Talking about why his wives had all left him, he would say: 'I really don't know why . . . they all got bored with me I guess. Tired of me. I really don't know.' It was the matinée idol-turned-misunderstood husband, the romantic lover betrayed.

It was also something of a parody of himself, and Grant, as usual, had used the lines, and the inflection, on the screen. In *North by Northwest*, the thriller he made with Hitchcock in 1959, Eva Marie Saint asks 'What happened to the first two marriages?'

'My wives divorced me,' replies the character played by Grant.

'Why?'

'They said I led too dull a life.'

It was in Grant's nature, however, to be publicly generous about his former wives. Whether or not in reality the final separation was always actually made by the woman, it became his stock response to insist that it was they who had abandoned him, and not him them. The suggestion, understood implicitly but never spelt out, was that he had somehow failed to measure up to their very high expectations and that they had probably been right to go. Each one, leaving, left behind her some kind of valedictory testimonial.

Grant's first three wives were all astonishingly alike in physical appearance, slim, cool, slightly pert blondes with an aura of high society and a promise of humour behind their rather wry expressions. His first marriage, to Virginia Cherrill, in 1934, was the shortest, lasting barely seven months. She departed, saying: 'I am in love with my husband, and have been very unhappy over our inability to adjust to our differences.' Virginia Cherrill had been married twice before. Not long after she and Grant were divorced in the Los Angeles superior court, she returned to England and married the Earl of Jersey. Grant's only comment was: 'No more marriages for me.'

In 1942, seven years later, Grant married Barbara Hutton. The relationship started in generosity and excitement, with Grant declaring that it would be him rather than America's richest heiress who would be buying the groceries, but that 'If she wants to buy diamond overshoes, that is her privilege.' Two years later they had separated.

The verdict, from both sides, was just as generous. 'Cary Grant had no title, and of my four husbands, he is the one I loved most,' Barbara Hutton later declared. 'He was so sweet, so gentle, it didn't work out, but I loved him.'

Grant quickly capped that: 'I was more interested in my work than I should have been, I suppose. She's a wonderful woman.'

The years with Betsy Drake, his third wife, were more complicated. For one thing the marriage lasted a remarkably long time, from Christmas 1949 till the day she went into the courts in Santa Monica in 1962 and sued for divorce on grounds of mental cruelty. 'I left Cary,' she commented, 'but physically he'd left me long ago.'

'Betsy,' said Grant, with by now predictable courtesy, 'was good for me.'

The two remained close friends. Indeed, of all his first four wives, friends were unanimous in agreeing that his marriage to Betsy Drake had been the happiest, and the one with the best chance of lasting. Had it not been for his unfortunate relationship with Sophia Loren during the filming of *The Pride and the Passion* in Spain, they would say, it need never have come to an end. To Weaver, in the course of their long association, Grant occasionally expressed his regrets at the end of the marriage. Betsy, he would say, had been both immensely intelligent and fun to be with; they had had good times together; she had taught him a lot. (Betsy Drake never remarried. Instead, she chose to make a career for herself in the academic world, taking a degree in psychology, and later doing postgraduate work at Stanford. Grant had left her very rich, not only with generous alimony payments and a house not far from his own, but ample residuals from several of his movies.)

Then there was Grant's fourth marriage, to a girl markedly younger than he was (a thirty-five-year difference in their ages.) It was the Virginia Cherrill pattern all over again; a bare two years this time and those rent by squabbles and ill feeling. The end, this time, was acrimonious, but once again, Grant was civil about his ex-wife, refusing, always, to speak ill of her.

Four marriages in a little over thirty years and just one child: it was hardly surprising that Grant took to commenting ironically that he would have been far better off with one wife and four daughters. Four marriages that ended, each of them, with Grant accused of mental cruelty, indifference, of appearing bored with his wife, and bored with her friends. (Not that anyone paid any attention. The public neither listened nor chose to believe that Grant could be a difficult man to live with. On the screen, he remained as desirable as he had ever been.) His record as a husband, however, was not good. The question was: why did he keep marrying, and why did the marriages go wrong?

Somewhere along the line, Grant himself came up with an answer. It was his mother's fault. By deserting him when he was nine, she had effectively conditioned him to anticipate and therefore precipitate desertion by his wives. 'I was making the mistake,' he once told one of the many reporters who clamoured round him, trying to prise out of him details about his private life, 'of thinking that each of my wives was my mother.' As if to bring the point home, he would say, speaking of his brief marriage to Virginia Cherrill, 'my possessiveness and fear of losing her brought about the very condition I feared: the loss of her.'

Certainly, few people can ever have suffered such a traumatic experience of separation as Grant did when, without warning, his mother vanished one day when he was at school. The decision not to explain to the boy what had happened was a typically Victorian one, and linked to the shame most middle- and working-class people felt about mental illness. But no stigma could have had a more devastating effect than the uncertainty that came with not knowing what had happened to his mother, and the hopes, constantly dashed, that she might suddenly reappear, unannounced, with as little fanfare as had accompanied her departure. For the first few months after her disappearance, the small boy, walking home from school, must have wondered whether or not he would find his mother miraculously returned to the house as he opened the front door.

Grant was never to talk freely to anyone about those years of adjustment, though the intensity which he brought to his experiments with LSD were a measure of his need to understand the past. After the sessions were over, and he had stopped taking the drug, he would have only generous things to say about his parents. 'I learned that my dear parents, products of *their* parents, could know no better than they knew, and began to remember them only for the most useful, the best, the wisest of their teachings.' What he did not say was how he had been thinking of them up until that moment.

Grant was in his thirties, a renowned Hollywood star, rich, with friends, fans, and a life utterly new and utterly different from that of the backstreets of Bristol, when an English lawyer wrote to tell him that his mother was in fact alive. The matter had been sparked off by the death of his father, Elias, after two operations, and the question as to who would now support her had been raised. Grant, her only child, was the only one who could make that decision, and Grant therefore had to be told the truth. It was a moment of anguish for him. For over twenty years he had imagined her dead, forced himself to accept the fact that he had no mother. Now, long after the process of adjustment had been completed, he had to reverse it, start again, repeat the years over in his mind, this time fitting in the existence of a mother, and with the added pain of realizing how destructive and distressing those years must have been for her. It was a challenge to his powers of understanding possibly no less hard to handle than the one of separation from her had been in the first place. And it was made harder by the fact that, even while she was with him when he was a small boy, she had never been very demonstrative towards him, and that one of his few vivid memories of her was of being pushed impatiently aside when he leaned forward to kiss her.

From that day on, however, Grant behaved like a dutiful son. Except for an unavoidable break during the war years, he took to crossing the Atlantic every year to visit her in Bristol, timing his journey, when work permitted, to coincide with her birthday in February. If he never managed to forge more than a pretence at a relationship with her, Grant can hardly be blamed. At thirty-five he was not the same person that he had been at nine. Nor was Elsie the same: twenty years in a mental hospital had done its bit in eroding a personality already weakened by unhappiness. The surprising thing was that it hadn't destroyed it altogether.

By the time Weaver came to work for Grant in the mid-1960s, Elsie Kingdon Leach was already living in a nursing home in Clifton, Bristol's more elegant suburb. The years spent on her own in a house bought for her by Grant after her release from Bristol's Victorian asylum had passed remarkably smoothly, but as she reached her seventies it had become obvious that she needed regular care. The Clifton Nursing Home, a handsome, quarry-stone Georgian town house, with magnificent views over the gorge, might not have seemed to be an obvious setting for an extremely eccentric old lady, but it was a comfortable and pleasant place to be, and Grant had the money and the influence to ensure that she was kept there.

At least once a year Grant and Weaver would fly to London, then pick up a car for the two-hour drive to Bristol. They would check into the Grand Spa Hotel, a little further down the hill towards the centre of the old trading city, with its own spectacular views over the gorge, and then go and visit Elsie. Grant would arrive with gifts, early daffodils if his visit managed to coincide with her birthday, and samples of Fabergé products.

Their relationship, by the late 1960s, was not an easy one. The jokes and memories the two had shared during her first years of liberty were fading as age began to dull her memory and fray her temper, though physically she was still exceptionally sprightly, a small, active, once beautiful woman with bright eyes and a beaked nose. Weaver, who usually waited in the car, noticed that Grant, so ebullient at the moment of arrival, would emerge from the nursing home door with a grim look on his face and remain terse for some hours. For the public, the actor laid on the sunniest of descriptions of these visits, repeating how vital his discovery of his mother had been to his happiness. After having taken her a fur coat one day, he joked with reporters about whether or not the gift was ecologically proper. But to Weaver, it was apparent that he found his mother's indifference towards him hard to take, just as she possibly found his sudden reappearance and kindness difficult to accept. 'What do you want from me now?' Grant repeated to Weaver a remark that his mother had made to him during the course of one visit.

'It's because I love you that I come and see you,' he had apparently replied.

Then, he said to Weaver, her voice had filled with scorn. 'Oh, *you*. . .' as if everything that he was trying to do was somehow ridiculous and totally unimportant to her. Another day, she berated

122

him for allowing his hair to go grey, saying that it aged her, and telling him petulantly that he should dye it.

Grant took her many criticisms with as much good temper and equanimity as he could, but Weaver sensed, as the years passed and the old lady grew increasingly senile, that he was finding the immense gap between them ever harder to bridge.

To relieve his distress during these days spent in Bristol, Grant would take Weaver off to see the local sights. One day they paid a visit to the Hippodrome in the centre, the theatre which had first fired Grant's imagination. They went backstage and talked to the manager and the performers and Grant was plainly happy to be able to show off all the gold and plush and recall the adventures of his early years, now some half-century past.

In January 1973, when Grant was in Beverly Hills, his cousin Maggie, who had been so kind and devoted to the old lady for the many years since her release from the asylum, rang to tell him that his mother was dead. Weaver took the call and went to fetch Grant to the phone, but Grant refused to come, preferring to let Weaver receive the details of her death and discuss with Maggie the funeral arrangements. The three-sided conversation was uneasy, and, Weaver felt, bizarre. Maggie, from Bristol, wanted to discuss flowers and the kind of service she was to arrange; Grant, from Los Angeles, seemed only interested in making clear that there was to be no announcement at all about his mother's death, so that he could attend her funeral in privacy. 'No hearse,' he kept repeating. 'Why can't we have a cart or something?' And, 'Above all, no flowers and no ceremony.'

The day of the funeral dawned gloomy beyond description. A heavy cloud of fog hung low over Bristol, and rain fell steadily throughout the day. It was extremely cold. Grant and Weaver, who had crept unnoticed into the city that morning, followed the pallbearers as they carried the body from the hearse to the graveside. The casket was pine, without ornament of any kind. There were no flowers. Only four people came to pay their last respects to Elsie Kingdon Leach, whose life up until the age of ninety-six had been spent entirely within the confines of a small

English city, though her son was one of the most famous of all living movie stars. At the graveside there were only Grant and Weaver and Maggie and her husband. As the coffin was lowered into the ground, Grant leaned over, took from Maggie's hands the single rose she was carrying, and laid it on the lid.

Afterwards the four mourners went back to have tea in Maggie's house. Grant was subdued, but not sad. When he spoke of his childhood, Weaver noticed, his reminiscences were affectionate and full of pleasure, but it was only when he spoke of his father that real warmth came into his voice.

Whatever Grant's ambiguities about his mother, and the harm that he felt that she had done to him, there was never any doubting of his affection for women. He needed their company, took pleasure in their presence, and seemed absurdly hopeful, as his four first marriages showed, of one day finding the ideal companion.

Between marriages, he formed friendships, had affairs, and went right on charming and bewitching all he came in contact with. His manner was invariably as charming off screen as on it: on aeroplanes he would lean over and ask a passing air hostess: 'Say "terrified". Now say "tissue". Now say "terrified tissue". "Faster".' At last the girl would be making sounds like 'care if I kiss you' and blushing violently.

But to Weaver, who spent so much time at his side, there often seemed something sad and brutal in these relationships, as if Grant were investing in them too many expectations and then felt bound to punish the women he took out for not being as he had hoped they would be. Being such a solitary figure at heart, Grant appeared to have no close men friends. As a result, the women he met and befriended became too important an ingredient in his life. And Grant was not an easy man to live with.

Some time after Dyan left for Malibu Beach, when the Beverly Grove Drive house was in presentable shape once more and Grant had ceased to feel so battered by the acrimoniousness of their last days together, he took to inviting girls out once more. The fact that he was getting on for seventy seemed utterly unimportant, both to him and to the women he took up with. If anything, he was better looking than he had been when younger, his appearance astonishingly unmarked by signs of age, a fact made all the more impressive by the very little exercise he took and the more or less total disregard he showed towards what he ate. Often Weaver would come across him after dinner, propped up on his bed and watching television, his hand dipping regularly into a box of chocolates by his side. For the younger man, ever worried about his weight, the sight was infuriating.

(This greed for chocolates was not without its comic interludes. Grant once recounted to McIntosh that he had been lying in bed one night watching television, with his date for the evening already asleep by his side, when a particularly gooey and indigestible chocolate jammed tight in his throat. Trying not to wake the girl, he fumbled his way out of the door leading to a corridor and the bathroom beyond in order to spit it out, when the security lock on the door snapped shut, leaving him in the pitch dark and trapped. 'I could just see the headlines next day,' he reported, laughing, to McIntosh. 'Leading male ex-movie star found naked in hallway, choked to death on a chocolate.')

There were, not surprisingly, no problems for Grant in finding companions for his evenings. Even if he shied away from close friendships, he had an immense acquaintance in Los Angeles, and whenever he did consent to go to a party there would be dozens of pressing women competing for his attentions. And because he was fond of women, and valued their company, he was quick to detect ones he might like, even in crowds. Crossing a hotel lobby with Weaver or McIntosh, Grant would suddenly catch sight of some exceptionally pretty woman as she stood waiting or reading a paper. 'Go and ask her if she would like to have dinner with an ageing movie star,' he would say, half seriously, half teasingly to his companions.

Usually, though, nothing happened. Weaver and McIntosh, loath to become involved, would drift away from Grant's side and manage to be somehow occupied elsewhere until the lady had vanished. Occasionally, however, one or the other would be trapped by Grant, and despite protestations and acute embarrassment, would find themselves despatched to pay court for him to a totally strange woman about whom none of them knew anything. There were few rebuttals, particularly once the woman had been convinced that it was really Cary Grant who was inviting her out to dinner and not the gimmick of a pushy stranger. Being Cary Grant, he was of course not a stranger: his face, his voice, his manner, his charm, even his clothes, were immensely familiar. Unless the woman was married, she nearly always accepted.

Dinners with these passing ladies usually took place, when Grant was in Los Angeles, at home. Since the actor continued to make front-page headlines whenever he was seen in public, the prospects of conducting a romantic courtship across a candle-lit table in an exclusive restaurant were negligible. In any case, the terrace of his house, under its fluted and domed Venetian canopy, with a view of the lights of Los Angeles stretching for miles below and around, was a pleasant place for an intimate supper. Less pleasant, perhaps, especially for Weaver, was Grant's insistence that his companion return to the city at some point during the night. Often it fell to Weaver to have to wait up until Grant decided to declare the evening over, so that he could drive the girl home. Dawn would be breaking as he turned the Rolls back down into the drive again.

These passing friends became a regular component of Grant's life in the late 1960s and throughout most of the 1970s, though a great deal of energy and concentration went on keeping their existence and their names out of the newspapers. Some, being celebrities in their own right, welcomed the secrecy. Grant and Raquel Welch shared a love of special sweet butter and cold meat sandwiches, bought from a delicatessen called Monaco in the San Fernando Valley, and eaten in private in front of her television set in Beverly Hills. But not all Grant's women companions took so warmly to the somewhat cavalier fashion in which they were being treated in public, particularly when their relationship with Grant seemed to them at least to be showing signs of becoming satisfactorily more permanent.

Maureen Donaldson was a twenty-eight-year-old writer for

movie magazines when she met Grant for the first time. She was English, with a round face, very regular features, and long, straight hair. But apart from her pretty face there was absolutely nothing about her that fitted at all with Grant's usually rather exigent taste in well-turned-out women. She was bohemian in dress and manner, a determined child of the 1960s. She wore nothing but jeans and her hair hung lankly around her shoulders; she much preferred to wear no shoes.

At first Grant was amused by her casualness. But he was also extremely cagey about being seen in her company. At a black-tie dinner in Beverly Hills, at which Grant was officiating and therefore sitting up at a table on a dais at one end of the hall, Maureen was put to sit next to Weaver at the far end, with the clear implication that she was Weaver's girlfriend.

In time, Weaver became aware that Maureen was growing increasingly irritated with the restrictions put upon her. But for a while at least, she chose to humour him. When they started spending more time together, and he protested that he could not be seen with her unless she dressed rather more elegantly, she meekly agreed to accompany the obliging Weaver on a shopping expedition, from which she returned laden with a wardrobe of clothes considered respectable in Grant's eyes.

Now that she was far more fashionably dressed, Grant consented to take her with him to various dinners and lunch engagements of a more formal kind. Maureen pretended to be grateful, obliging. The first few passed without a hitch. Then came her moment of revenge. She waited until an especially formal occasion, when she was seated next to the football star Joe Namath. Her neighbour turned to her: 'Miss Donaldson,' he asked politely, 'what brings you to Los Angeles?'

'Oh,' she replied jokingly, 'I'm a tart. Cary Grant brought me here.'

What was surprising to Weaver in fact was that Grant was not caught out more often. Though he did take precautions – changing cars, avoiding restaurants, refusing to take holidays – there were inevitably times when he grew exceedingly bored with trying to be discreet, and then Weaver would scan the local newspapers in an agony of apprehension for some terrible revelation.

It was the board meetings that most alarmed him. Grant was a conscientious director and seldom missed any of the MGM, Fabergé or Western Airlines scheduled meetings; but he did not like to go alone. McIntosh, who accompanied him, was astonished to find that Grant thought nothing of flying into the city in which the meeting was to take place, with a girl in tow, almost invariably an air hostess from the airline on which he had just been flying.

The day came when Grant, whether irritated by his fastidious and complacent fellow-directors, or simply remembering, in a high-spirited way, some of the more caddish and daring of the roles he had played in his early films, decided to play a monumental joke. On this occasion, he solemnly walked into the board room where a meeting was about to start with a very pretty girl at his side. 'This,' he announced pleasantly, 'is Miss Smith.' The various men present shuffled awkwardly to their feet and muttered their names. Grant continued to smile benignly. Miss Smith remained sedately at his side.

After what seemed an interminable period of time in which the directors murmured to each other and shuffled their papers about and Grant and Miss Smith exchanged casual small talk, McIntosh felt that the time had come when the meeting could no longer be delayed. He approached Grant and whispered uneasily in his ear: 'What are you going to do with Miss Smith?'

'Oh! She's staying with me of course,' replied Grant in fulsome tones, smiling agreeably. 'Why doesn't she sit right down here at my side?' His gestures, his voice, his wry laughter were all straight from an early Cukor role.

The directors were appalled but helpless. They took their seats, some trying not to laugh, some obviously outraged, and the meeting began. Grant threw himself into it with gusto, with Miss Smith beaming approvingly at him by his side. Anyone scrutinizing the bald notes of the meeting afterwards would have been mystified to find included the name 'Miss Smith' among 'those present' with no explanation whatsoever as to her presence.

These, however, were passing affairs. None were very serious and none lasted for more than a few encounters. Invariably, it was Grant who grew bored. But, as Weaver observed, he was not always very kind in the way he parted from his dates. There would be scenes, recriminations, and then the lady, if mildly truculent or resistant, would be evicted.

Grant did, however, enter into one relationship in the late 1960s that meant a great deal to him and might very easily have turned into something more lasting. That it ended in disaster says as much of the extraordinary wariness of Grant as for the role that luck plays in relationships of all kinds.

Arabella – this is not her real name – was the young widow of an extremely successful Hollywood producer who had died some years before, leaving her rich and well connected. She was French by birth, exceedingly pretty, and greatly liked by everyone who knew her. She and Grant became close friends soon after they were first introduced, by mutual friends, in Palm Springs (though their friendship got off to an inauspicious start when Grant decided to show her around his decaying house and an enormous mirror hanging in the bathroom, as dilapidated as everything else in the place, crashed and shattered into a thousand fragments at her feet).

At first the relationship seemed full of charm. Arabella, like Grant, was by nature neither very gregarious nor very fond of parties, and the two had many pleasant evenings on the terrace of the Beverly Grove Drive house. Since Arabella owned an apartment in Paris, they made a trip to France together, taking Weaver with them. Ever afterwards, Weaver remembered the holiday with delight. Grant had been at his most charming, generous, good-tempered, and full of suggestions for what his young secretary should see and do on his first visit to Europe.

One day, in the pouring rain, the three of them sheltering companiably under an enormous umbrella, they made a pilgrimage to a flat Grant had once lived in belonging to Somerset Maugham. Another, they walked down the Champs-Elysées, with Grant pointing out the sights, and Arabella adding funny stories of her own. It was obvious that he was very happy.

But Arabella, like Grant, was nervous and slightly touchy, and she soon became very dependent on him. Grant always found dependency difficult. Scenes and rows developed with Arabella complaining of his lack of affection – shades of Barbara Hutton and Betsy Drake – and Grant became visibly annoyed by her demands. Often Weaver would find himself chauffeuring the tearful Arabella down the mountain back to her own house in the morning with all her belongings in suitcases in the boot, vowing never to speak to Grant again, only to have to return that same evening to collect her and bring her back up the mountain once more. It was an unusually fraught relationship.

Several uneasy months passed. Then the day came when Grant was due to leave for a business meeting in New York, to be followed by a trip to London. There were no plans for Arabella to go with him.

As Grant was packing, his attention as ever held by a desire to fold his clothes immaculately in their proper creases inside his suitcase, an argument broke out between them. Weaver's younger brother, David, chanced unwittingly on a moment of hysteria when Arabella appealed to Grant not to leave her behind.

When Grant and Weaver reached the airport, some time later that afternoon, Grant asked Weaver to ring home, saying that he had a terrible premonition that Arabella might do something foolish to herself. There was a telephone in the Ambassador's Lounge and Weaver soon dialled the house. Instantly, David picked up the receiver at the other end, a note of panic in his voice. 'Thank God you've rung. You must come back. Arabella has taken a lot of pills. She's unconscious.'

Weaver hurried to find Grant, assuming that all their plans would now be cancelled. Grant, however, did not seem disposed to take the matter very seriously. He hesitated, then said he would fly on to New York for his meeting alone, as scheduled, but that Weaver should return to the Beverly Hills house and check that all was well.

When Weaver reached the house some forty minutes later, he found Arabella comatose on the stone floor of the sitting room,

David having been unable on his own to shift the unconscious body into a more comfortable position. Together, the two men heaved and pulled and between them managed to lay her out on a rug, and then covered her with blankets. There was no question of lifting her on to a bed; her inert body, acting as a dead weight, was simply too heavy even for two men.

While Weaver and his brother sat waiting for the doctor, their apprehension grew. They tried slapping Arabella's face, then sticking a pin in her arm, in the hope that she would produce some sort of indication, other than breathing, that she was really alive, but the girl never moved.

Now began, for Weaver, a time of hideous confusion; later, he was to remember its black comedy side, but as one disaster followed fast upon another, all he could think of was that Arabella was going to die. Her skin was turning blue and there was something definitely peculiar about her breathing. After what seemed an immensely long time, the doctor's car drew up at the gates; he inspected Arabella, noted her by now very purple skin, and summoned an ambulance; he then disappeared into the night.

The ambulance, too, took its time in coming, and when the driver emerged finally through the front door he turned out to be a man of almost monstrous appearance, with a tic in one eye, and the look of the Hunchback of Notre Dame. As the four men, Weaver, his brother, the driver, and a hospital orderly, struggled to haul the body into the back of the ambulance the siren went off and jammed: the wail kept up, without a pause, for the entire duration of the journey to the hospital.

That might indeed have gone smoothly, had it not been for the fact that the driver turned in error on to the freeway in the wrong direction, so that they had to travel for some miles in the wrong lane with cars streaming towards them honking frantically. The detour the ambulance was then obliged to take took considerable time and Weaver, watching Arabella as she lay on the stretcher in the back, noticed that her face was turning an even deeper shade of puce. He pointed this out to the orderly who promptly fitted an oxygen mask over her face and switched on the supply, only for the hose to snap

131

in two, beyond repair. Time seemed, to Weaver, to stop. He sat, frozen in horror, watching as her breathing became more irregular, while the driver hooted, the siren wailed, and the ambulance jerked forward, a few yards at a time, embroiled in a stream of commuter traffic leaving the city after work.

Matters grew horribly bizarre when they reached the hospital. A doctor, peering into the back of the ambulance, agreed with Weaver that a constriction seemed to be building up in the girl's throat and started to massage it, while shrugging his shoulders and saying, 'What's the point? To look at her, I'd say she was done for anyway.' A new oxygen apparatus was produced and a new mask fitted over her face, but this one failed too, as did a second, on the emergency ward. That night her lungs threatened to pack up and Weaver, who had spent the evening desperately trying to reach members of her family, now contacted a sister in St Louis, Missouri, who gave her permission for a tracheotomy to be performed.

For two weeks, Arabella was kept in intensive care. Weaver stayed with her, sleeping at night in a wicker chair by the side of her bed. Grant followed developments closely by phone from New York.

She was in hospital for many weeks. Long before she was ready to leave, Grant returned to Los Angeles. But something in the whole business had sickened him and he adamantly refused to go near the hospital, or even to send Arabella flowers, making a joke of it over the telephone to her – she was by now out of intensive care and in a private room of her own – that flowers would only absorb all the much-needed oxygen in her room.

When she did finally emerge from her hospital bed, she was full of fury and hatred against Grant but absolutely unresolved about whether or not to see him again. Grant solved this for her, by saying that he didn't wish to see her again. So she summoned Weaver to come and visit her, and wept on his shoulder, cursing and bewailing Grant at the same time. She never did see him again. Not long afterwards, she remarried. Grant, when he was told the news, appeared unmoved. He had successfully put the entire episode firmly out of his mind.

9
Shangri-la

Early in 1970 William McIntosh received a call from a Chicago businessman called Donald J. Barrett. The two men were already associates, McIntosh's production companies being suppliers of Barrett's electronic factories. The Chicago millionaire had a proposition to put to him: what would he say to coming in on the construction of an Irish-American community village in Ireland, on the banks of the Shannon–Fergus rivers, some fifteen minutes from the International Airport, to which prosperous Americans who had roots in the old country would retire? Barrett already had his eye on a property, he told McIntosh. It was a 555-acre site, consisting of a number of farmers' smallholdings between the villages of Ballynacally and Kildysart. It had a derelict two-storey Georgian house, ideal for expansion into a clubhouse, the right lie of land for a championship golf course, and some of the most magical and unspoilt scenery left in the world. McIntosh was impressed.

Furthermore, Barrett said to him, the consortium needed a figurehead, someone who would lend his name and enthusiasm to the project. Did he have any ideas?

Yes, replied McIntosh, he did. There was his friend Cary Grant. Why couldn't he do for Shannonside – as the scheme had by now been christened – precisely what he had done for Fabergé?

Grant needed little convincing. There was something in the idea of an untouched landscape, bordering onto the Atlantic, with the fresh gusts of unpolluted wind blowing in from the sea, where people could come and cleanse their souls, a sort of return to Eden, that appealed to his expatriate's nature. Better than anyone, perhaps, he knew the appeal of going home, the lure of being able to return to where you had started from. 'Yes,' he said immediately to McIntosh, 'I'll come in on the venture. What's more, I'll invest in it.' With which he wrote out a cheque for $10,000. 'But,' he added, 'we must now go and look at it.'

Some weeks later the two men met at Heathrow Airport. McIntosh was flying in from America, Grant had been to pay his mother a visit in Bristol. Amid the usual crowds and hysteria that surrounded all Grant expeditions, they caught a small plane to Shannon and by that evening were installed in a former turreted baronial hall, once the seat of Lord Ichiquin, now the hotel Dromoland Castle owned by a West Virginian called Bernard McDonough. The hotel itself could have come straight from a Hollywood set: a grey papier mâché backdrop for Robin Hood, set in Versailles, with formal gardens and, beyond, rivers, lakes, and woods stretching for miles.

Shannonside, as Grant discovered next morning, was indeed a spectacular site. The 555 acres consisted of a gently rolling landscape of fields, meadows, and copses, with the River Shannon looping its way through the middle down to the Atlantic coast beyond. On one side of the river were the remains of the former manor house, complete with outhouses, barns, and stables. On a soft Irish morning, with a haze rising off the sea, and the greys and greens of the land merging gently all around, it did indeed look like a corner of paradise.

On 9 September 1971, Grant became a formal director of the company at a board meeting in Chicago. He threw himself into the discussions with genuine enthusiasm, debating how best to allocate the parcels of land, what style to use to construct the estimated 2,100 cottages or garden flats, where to lay out a Pye Vavra golf course and stables. Then there was the matter of finance: the land had cost the company $555,000 and the finished venture was expected to come to some $30 million; $850,000 worth of shares now had to be issued and sold.

From the first, Grant treated the Shannonside project with

proprietorial affection. It was, he seemed to be indicating, *his*, in that he alone could really see the full measure of its beauty and its promise. When McIntosh moved to bring another film star friend, Jack Lemmon, into the consortium, Grant was appalled and rang to express his fear that stars like Lemmon would put off the sort of buyer he imagined Shannonside would attract, the 'sensible man who wants a good home for his children'.

'I think you must be very careful about bringing in these movie stars because you're going to wreck our project,' he said, sternly, over the telephone to McIntosh, wholly failing to see the irony in his position. 'Movie stars for that kind of project are not what you need. My age and my aura of dignity that you know I don't really have,' and here Grant laughed, '*are* suited to your project. But when you bring in Jack Lemmon and all those names of course the newspaperman is going to pick it up because for him it's colourful. . .' What no one thought to mention was that Grant himself was planning to take Raquel Welch to Shannonside to lay the foundation stone for the holiday village. Despite Grant's objections, Lemmon did come in on the deal – to the tune of $20,000, double Grant's own investment.

Over the next few years the Shannonside Company provided Grant with a lot of fun. Usually in the company of William McIntosh, he would cross the Atlantic from time to time to watch progress on the property as small stone walls arose criss-crossing the site, as an underground heating system was sunk, as foundations were laid, and the bones of three small separate villages, at different ends of the estate, were mapped out.

Invariably elegantly dressed, in clothes that came straight from London and Beverly Hills, he would stride over the land, pointing out to newcomers the sweeping main gateway, or sketching for them, with his hands, a broad map of the buildings and driveways rising all around them. A young cameraman called Michael Taylor, who McIntosh had met in London, accompanied the party on one of their expeditions to Shannon and put together what McIntosh fondly referred to as Grant's 'last movie'. The film shows Grant on what he sometimes called his Shangri-la (possibly remembering the

legendary 'Pickfair' Shangri-la, built by his old hero Douglas
Fairbanks and Mary Pickford in the canyons above Beverly Hills),
surveying the rolling acres, gesticulating, smiling, arguing. It had
been McIntosh's idea to have such a movie, and at first Grant, who
had refused all screen appearances and interviews for many years,
had been extremely reluctant to co-operate, pushing the hapless
young photographer rather brusquely to one side. But then he
relented and laughed and threw himself into the work, pausing
from time to time to turn director and show the young man how
such a film should be made. When it was done, Grant turned to
McIntosh, 'You better lock that up,' he said. 'That's the last film
ever shot of me.' Never shown, the film remains locked up today
in McIntosh's safe.

The Shannonside project took on an additional pleasure for
Grant when, some two years after he had first become involved, the
board of directors agreed that Grant and McIntosh, for their pains,
should be given plots of land of their own on which they could put
up their respective houses at their own expense. Grant was
overjoyed, all the more so as he felt that he had earned his reward
in terms of the considerable publicity he had engineered for the
venture. Asked to pick his own site, he flew to Shannon, paced the
555 acres, and settled on a five-acre plot overlooking the golf course
and near the water. Already he knew just how the house would
look: a verandah the entire length of the building on the river side,
a bedroom wing for him at one end and another for Jennifer at the
other, but no dining room. 'You fashion your home,' he told
McIntosh, 'so you may eat in comfort in any room.' On that visit
Grant radiated *bonhomie*, pausing to drink at a local pub with
villagers who now regularly turned out to greet him, and having tea
with the foreman, Michael Geary, in his grey stone cottage.

Jennifer was always in his thoughts, and much of the time, when
not out on a tour of inspection of the rolling acres, he would be
dreaming up presents to take home to her, or combing through
Kildysart's meagre shops for souvenirs, or sitting upstairs in his
suite in Dromoland Castle writing letters to her. A letter went off
by the early post every morning: one day it would include a riddle;

the next, the answer to it. Before posting them off, Grant would try the latest offering on whomever he happened to find himself with at the time. 'What,' he asked the assembled company at breakfast one morning, 'has ninety-nine legs and goes thump, thump, thump?' There was much laughter but not a satisfactory reply. 'A centipede with a wooden leg,' Grant announced triumphantly. There seemed to be no end to his supply of riddles, nor to the pleasure that he took in finding them.

These new business commitments in Ireland drew Grant, for so many years a virtual stranger to his own country, increasingly often to London. Though there were obviously more convenient direct flights from Los Angeles to Shannon, Grant usually preferred to use the occasion of a visit to the site as a pretext for a few days' pause in the capital, to shop for clothes and shoes, to eat at restaurants he particularly liked, like the Guinea in Bruton Place, to buy New Mown Hay, a toilet water from Floris he had conceived a particular passion for, and to see a couple of old friends. It was a strange return for a boy who had left his home country as an apprentice music-hall comedian some fifty years before.

Because of their Shannonside partnership, William McIntosh was a frequent companion on Grant's London jaunts. The two men had a particularly relaxed friendship, with a shared love of good food and a similar taste in jokes and slapstick. (Grant was a gourmet and loved his food, eyeing the dessert trolley in restaurants with undisguised longing. On board the plane crossing the Atlantic, he would eat as much caviar as he could persuade the airline company to provide him with, exchanging his portion firmly with McIntosh's if he sensed that his share was somehow the smaller.)

It was over dinners in London together that McIntosh occasionally heard stories of Grant's past life as an actor though he was noticeably reticent about discussing a part of his life that he now considered totally finished. One anecdote, that Grant was extremely fond of and that seemed to conjure up something of his love of practical jokes, concerned the filming of *Gunga Din* in 1939. The cast, which included Douglas Fairbanks Jr, Victor McLaglen, and Joan Fontaine, had been billeted in tents on location in the mountains some way from Hollywood. *Gunga Din* was an epic of Kiplingesque colonial India, with Grant playing a cockney soldier called Archibald Cutter (another time he fooled about on screen with his real name). One night, as they had gathered with the rest of the crew to discuss the following day's shooting, Grant crept back to his tent, collected a portable radio, one of the first ever seen and which he had just been given, and placed it behind the tent where everyone was sitting talking quietly. Then he flicked the switch to 'on', having first set the volume at 'maximum'. The sound, exploding out across the wilderness, caused pandemonium. Cast and crew scattered in amazement and terror. Grant, tears of laughter running down his face, finally gathered them all back together to show off his new toy. It was vaudeville and slapstick – all that, on screen and off, he loved best.

Based at the Connaught Hotel just off Grosvenor Square, Grant and McIntosh would make forays into the best menswear shops, and stock up on suits and sweaters for their return to California. Grant, as one of the world's best-dressed men, was frequently offered discounts. On one visit to London, in the very early 1970s, Grant was invited by Sir Charles Abrahams, chairman of Aquascutum, to lend his support to a charitable venture by posing for a photograph wearing an Aquascutum suit. In return, Grant was offered a substantial discount on anything he and McIntosh chose to buy from the firm. Like two companionable schoolboys on an illicit spree, they visited Aquascutum in Regent Street and selected for themselves entire new wardrobes, made up for them by the head tailor in materials they had picked out. To these, Grant added a couple of new dinner jackets.

There was something about these semi-free offers that never lost its appeal for Grant, as if an austere and impoverished childhood had left him with a hunger for gifts that could never quite be appeased. It was the same, McIntosh noted, with meals. Grant would very rarely pay a bill. If Fabergé was not covering the expenses of any particular trip, then Grant was always happy to accept the restaurant manager's almost invariable insistence that the meal be on the house. For the restaurant, Grant's presence alone was worth an incalculable amount in free publicity; for Grant, these were the well-earned rewards of stardom.

There was, in fact, about these brief stays in London, something that brought out the boyish streak in Grant, something that reminded McIntosh of the actor at his most raffish in his parts in *Mr Lucky* or *Holiday* so that he was constantly alert, making jokes, and seeking, somewhat restlessly, constant entertainment. Towards Weaver, who frequently accompanied him, he displayed an avuncular concern over clothes, and many of Grant's own excursions in search of cashmere sweaters from N. Peal in the Burlington Arcade, or a new jacket from a West End tailor, would be followed by expeditions to fit Weaver out in clothes pronounced by Grant to be suitably elegant. Grant seemed greatly to enjoy his role of mentor and tutor and took as many pains in making Weaver look good as he did with his own appearance.

For Weaver, all journeys with Grant, whatever their nature or purpose, had their worries. The crowds and the fans were only one threat to his peace of mind. Just as aggravating was the continual pilfering, on a small scale, that went on every time the actor moved from his own home, as hotel laundries deliberately failed to return monogrammed clothes, or hotel staff tried to make off with mementoes from the star's belongings. Weaver, on these occasions, turned watchdog, and was for ever counting, for ever replenishing severely depleted stocks of handkerchiefs or socks, mysteriously vanished during the course of some journey.

He was severely handicapped in his occasional role of valet by Grant's habit, all part of the comic public persona fashioned by the actor in the course of so many romantic parts, of appearing exceedingly vague and chaotic with his personal belongings. So fastidious at home, so meticulous when it came to a perfectly packed suitcase – his luggage was designed specially for him by Fulton's in New York, to his exact specifications – Grant turned rapidly into a parody of the hopeless and bumbling traveller once he was on the move. In a plane, glasses, sweaters, address books, jackets, newspapers, and business papers would fly about and fall in a jumble on to the floor and in the aisles, only to be gathered up by obliging air hostesses, always hovering at Grant's shoulder. Disembarking, for the attendant Weaver and McIntosh, would be a charming nightmare of forgotten belongings, mislaid possessions, and untidy hand luggage, as Grant, rumpled, glasses slipping from his nose, a look of almost beatific charm on his face, and smiling with wry self-deprecation, in a perfect imitation of any one of fifty film parts, would emerge stumbling through customs.

In London, as in Los Angeles, Grant seemed to have few close friends, though he was a regular lunch guest in the Albany set of rooms owned by Fleur Cowles, the painter and society hostess. Usually, as in California, he preferred the company of those he had brought with him, and shied away in horror from all suggestion of any kind of public engagement.

One invitation he could not refuse, however, was to Buckingham Palace. Despite his position as doyen of the British film colony in Hollywood, where he was always much in demand for visiting British dignitaries, Grant was not invited to the palace until the early 1970s. When the invitation to attend a benefit dinner given by Prince Philip in aid of wildlife conservation came, Grant decided to use the event as a reason for paying another visit to Shannonside and to combine the two in a longer British holiday. He could, in any case, hardly have refused this particular summons: the gala dinner was to be televised, and Fabergé had announced that it would be sponsoring the showing of the film on American television.

As it happened, the Buckingham Palace dinner became the centre of a particularly bitter row with Arabella, still at that period Grant's regular companion. Grant had been informed that he might bring a guest with him to the Palace and had consequently asked Arabella if she would like to accompany him. Arabella, who was in Paris at the time, was delighted, but asked Grant, who had phoned to relay the invitation from California, whether he would bring with him by plane across the Atlantic a special dress that her old friend Ursula Andress was going to lend her for the occasion. Grant refused. It was not perhaps entirely surprising: his years with Dyan Cannon, with her penchant for enormous travelling wardrobes, had given him a loathing, amounting at times to a kind of phobia, for anything but the most restrained amount of luggage. Even Weaver was severely rationed in what he was allowed to take with him when they were together. The prospect of an additional dress, and heaven knows what else, was not likely to pass Grant's rigid set of rules.

Arabella, however, was not prepared to be defeated quite so easily. From Grant, she turned to the unfortunate Weaver, who had none of his employer's strength and determination in refusing favours, and eventually succumbed to her blandishments. The box containing the dress was delivered to him one day surreptitiously when Grant was out, and Weaver was appalled to see it consisted of an immense, voluminous frock, covered in sequins the size of dollar pieces, which crackled and clinked together like a chest of smuggler's treasure. With some misgivings, he packed it away in his case between two layers of shirts.

At Heathrow Airport in London, Weaver did his best to become separated from Grant as they neared the customs' officers. The harder he tried to offer his place in the queue to fellow-passengers from Los Angeles, the more they politely stood aside, so that when the moment came to open the suitcases, Weaver found himself helplessly standing alongside Grant. As his bag opened to reveal the enormous, flamboyant, multicoloured, and sequined gown, Grant fixed him with a furious glare. Later, at the Berkeley Hotel where they were staying, Grant bawled him out severely, furious beyond all logical reason that Weaver should have been so deftly manipulated by Arabella.

His fury lasted well after Arabella herself arrived from Paris with a streaming cold and in an extremely irritable mood, with none of the abject apology that Grant was hoping to see. That evening Grant's Bristol cousins, Maggie and Eric Leach, came into the Berkeley for a drink and Arabella declared that she would retire to her bed and sulk. Grant, always formal and particular at these events, hating all suggestion of vulgarity, all innuendo and indiscretion, chose to pretend that he had come to London on his own, with only Weaver to keep him company.

Just as the Leaches were preparing to leave, after an hour's agreeable talk about Bristol, the door to the bedroom burst open and Arabella slouched provocatively into the room, dressed only in a négligé. Long after the Leaches had left, in a flurry of embarrassment, Grant was still storming around the room, shouting at Arabella that there was no longer the slightest hope that she might accompany him to Buckingham Palace.

He kept his word. The next night while Arabella retired to bed and brooded, he went alone to the gala, which turned out to be an almost unique occasion, in that members of seventeen royal families were present at the Palace. The following morning, however, the British newspapers were united in their outrage at the whole event. Two hundred of the women guests had chosen to attend this fund-raising benefit for the protection of endangered species decked out in fur coats – leopard, tiger, sable, wolf. Clare Booth Luce, chairwoman of the leading charity, wore the most splendid fur of them all.

It was Grant's foible about excessive luggage that led indirectly to discussion about whether or not the actor should buy a share in a London apartment. Both the Connaught and the Berkeley were immensely agreeable places to stay, but as Grant took to crossing the Atlantic more regularly, so he longed for cupboards in which to hang his many suits without having the constant bother of packing and carrying them backwards and forwards. McIntosh, whose business life was much like Grant's, proposed that between them they should take one of the service flats run by the Grosvenor House Hotel on Park Lane, with one master suite and one secondary bedroom and bathroom. On subsequent visits to London, McIntosh spent a great deal of time setting up the arrangement, negotiating terms with the Grosvenor management and inspecting apartments as they fell vacant. When the moment came to sign, Grant's enthusiasm had mysteriously faded. He was not, McIntosh reflected a little bitterly, an entirely easy man to deal with.

As with the repairs on his house in Beverly Grove Drive, Grant often seemed possessed of sudden bouts of irrational anxiety, when he would believe himself the victim of dishonest workmen, lying officials, and opportunistic entrepreneurs. While friends sympathized with his fears, they felt powerless to intercede, especially as Grant held on to an opinion, once he had formed it, with extraordinary tenacity. The idea that suddenly appealed to him of owning a holiday house in Spain met with the same fate as many of his more adventurous plans.

While Shannonside was rising out of the Irish meadows, McIntosh bought for himself a plot of land in Marbella, in southern Spain, overlooking the sea. It was a charming, secluded spot, with two empty farmhouses, and what was more, it was remarkably cheap. Next to the plot stood another, similar in size, and just as private. McIntosh suggested to Grant that he should buy it.

Grant had a particular fondness for Spain, dating back to the days of filming *The Pride and the Passion*. He grew increasingly enthusiastic about the idea, and McIntosh duly went through the many labyrinthine steps necessary for such transactions under Spanish law. When the day came to exchange contracts he was not particularly surprised to learn that the price for each of the estates had in fact risen by $1,000. There were items he had overlooked in the negotiations, and at $8,500 for each plot of land, the deal was still remarkably good.

Grant, however, on hearing of the additional demand, was absolutely outraged. Over the phone, he told McIntosh that they were obviously being ripped off by greedy middlemen, and that on no account was he going to pay the extra thousand. McIntosh reasoned with him, pointed out all the advantages of the purchase, begged him to reconsider. But a sort of passionate integrity seemed to have seized Grant, who now insisted that whatever the outcome he would now never feel the same about the property. McIntosh was instructed to tear up Grant's cheque and to cancel the contract. (In time a Danish couple bought the estate that would have been Grant's, and McIntosh built himself a villa on his own land. In time, too, Grant's land became worth some twelve times the price he had, overcome with misplaced and irrational fears, considered preposterously high.)

143

By some quirk of chance, it was Grant who, of all the Shannonside directors, was the one who first heard the news that the company was in trouble. At the beginning of March 1974 he received a letter from Lawrence Crowley, newly appointed receiver of Shannonside Holdings Ltd. 'I should be obliged,' wrote Mr Crowley, 'if you would let me have details of any claim you may have against the company until the date of my appointment, the 18th February 1974.' Grant picked up the phone and rang McIntosh: was it possible that their venture had collapsed?

It was indeed possible. To raise capital the consortium had entered into an agreement with an American mortgage company, Associated Mortgage Investors or AMI, who, it was hoped, would put $6 million initially into the scheme and continue to fund it, step by step, providing the consortium agreed not to go elsewhere for any of the investment. In the event, AMI failed to raise the money, the bills mounted up in Shannon, the workmen were not paid, and the scheme had to declare itself bankrupt. A morass of legal difficulties now engulfed all operations and made it impossible for the consortium to turn to others for backing. As of now, the fate of the Shannonside project lies in the hands of the Dublin courts.

The collapse of Shannonside touched Grant financially not at all. He had long been an extremely rich man, with a fortune put at around $25 to $35 million, a house in Beverly Hills, a handsome royalty on the copyright of his movies still in his possession, as well as the incalculable perks provided by Fabergé in the shape of his penthouse at the Warwick in New York, the fleet of cars and aeroplane at his service, the travel expenses and the huge personal allowances. A loss of $10,000 down an Irish drain was scarcely going to affect all that. But it did come as a bitter blow to his private dreams.

A part of Grant's future was tied up in his vision of a tranquil Irish life, in the company of his daughter, living in a house specially created by him. In his mind he had seen himself there, growing old, coming to rest from time to time in a place of perfect peace. For Grant, it was a sad dream to abandon.

10

'The Façade of a Fellow Known as Cary Grant'

From Mae West to Katharine Hepburn, Ingrid Bergman to Grace Kelly, Marilyn Monroe to Irene Dunne, every renowned Hollywood actress for over thirty years did her best on celluloid to tempt, bewitch, and marry Cary Grant. Paid court to by one after another of the great ladies of the cinema, Grant is possibly the most seduced star ever to appear on screen. There was, in fact, scarcely an actress of standing who did not, at some point from the 1930s to the 1960s, play opposite to Grant. 'Why don't you come up sometime and see me? Come on up. I'll tell your fortune,' purred Mae West to the newly arrived ex-vaudeville actor in his first Hollywood success. Three decades later, Audrey Hepburn was still asking: 'Won't you come in for a minute? I don't bite, you know, unless it's called for.' As Pauline Kael wrote in her *New Yorker* profile: 'Cary Grant is the male love object.'

For the women who starred opposite him, there was really only one Cary Grant, and he was always desirable. He could be difficult and swaggering – as in *Mr Lucky*, when he took the role of unsuitable lover to Laraine Day; he could be absent-minded and a little pedantic – as when he was helping Katharine Hepburn catch her leopard in *Bringing up Baby*; he could even turn sly and manipulating – as when he was trying to entice Rosalind Russell back to work in *His Girl Friday*. But whatever his character, whatever nuance or inflection he adopted, however suitable or unsuitable he might be, there was always something a little elusive in his manner, so that women partners had to make the running,

145

convinced that deep down he really wanted them, but was not going to let anyone know it. For well over thirty years, laying claim to the title of longest-lived romantic lead in the history of the cinema, Grant was the lover to catch.

Some of his leading ladies appeared with him only once on screen – Marlene Dietrich, Jean Harlow, Jayne Mansfield, Sophia Loren, Marilyn Monroe. Others hit off some particular spark or note when paired with him and produced film after film – Katharine Hepburn, Irene Dunne, Ingrid Bergman. The women in the films changed; Grant did not. Though it is certainly arguable that, without them, there never would have been a Cary Grant at all. With the women came the image.

Yet, however close the association, however long-lasting the partnership, extremely few of these leading ladies ever became Grant's close or life-long friends. One or two, admittedly, went out on dates with him, like Rosalind Russell and Ginger Rogers. But mostly the relationships remained professional and remote. The actresses, when questioned about him, would usually say how much they had enjoyed acting with him, in that his sense of humour and his practical jokes injected a constant note of enjoyment into the weeks of shooting. Katharine Hepburn once described him as 'cocky, bouncy, nasally humorous'. For his part, Grant very rarely referred to his partners at all, saying loudly and often rather tetchily that it bored him to be questioned so much about which of his leading ladies he had most liked working with. In one of the few pronouncements he ever did make on the subject, he was drawn only on one of them. 'She taught me,' he said, referring to Katharine Hepburn, 'just about everything I know about comedy.' As on the subject of his wives, Grant preferred to remain silent about his leading ladies.

A very few did, of course, become good friends, even if Grant's somewhat distant brand of friendship grew more distant with the years, which meant that visits were exceedingly few and exceedingly far between. (Grant preferred the telephone to actual meetings, using it to keep in touch with friends from the past he now never saw. He spoke to Marilyn Monroe the night before she died, and later said to Weaver that he bitterly regretted not having tried harder to help her.) Rosalind Russell was one of the privileged handful; Grant had been best man at her wedding to Frederick Brisson at the beginning of the war and, after Jennifer's birth, she became one of the few old friends he chose to see. Ingrid Bergman was another. But it was still another Hitchcock leading lady, Grace Kelly, who became a truly close friend.

There had been an idea in the mid-1950s that Grant should buy the rights to *His Girl Friday*, in order to remake his earlier success with a new leading lady – Grace Kelly in place of Rosalind Russell. That suggestion had foundered. Instead he partnered Grace Kelly in *To Catch a Thief* for Hitchcock (for both of them, their third Hitchcock film), a comedy thriller about a retired cat burglar who comes out of retirement to help bait a thief who is imitating his style and making him the prime suspect for a series of spectacular jewel robberies. *To Catch a Thief* was filmed in the South of France, with Grant scrambling over rooftops – apparently entirely cured of his fear of heights – and falling in love with a young American heiress. Off the set, Grace Kelly was herself falling in love for real, with Prince Rainier, to whom she had just been introduced. Of all his Hollywood friendships, Grace Kelly became and remained the best, not least perhaps because she herself left Hollywood. Right up until her death in 1982 Grant was a regular visitor to Monaco, both as a guest of the Rainiers, and, in his capacity of former tightrope walker and acrobat, as one of the judges for the annual Monaco circus competition. Grant was one of the few Hollywood stars to attend her funeral.

It was when he reached his seventies that Cary Grant seemed to find a smoother course to his life. The confusions and anxieties that had threatened to overwhelm him with the break-up of his fourth marriage, the removal of his only daughter, and his self-imposed exile from the movies gradually evaporated, and with them disappeared the pernicketiness and the worst of the irrational bouts of indecision. He did not become easy to live with, but he seemed, once more, in control. Not long after his seventy-first birthday, he told a reporter: 'I have never been more myself than I am today. I pretended to be a certain kind of man on the screen, to be Cary Grant, and I more or less became that man in life. Now I can be Archie Leach again.'

It was, however, a very different Archie Leach from the gangling, apprehensive vaudeville juvenile who had boarded the RMS *Olympic* in Southampton fifty-five years before. The new Archie was rich and famous, and had evolved for himself a style of life that was both opulent and very much his own. Over decades of increasing prosperity he had formed tastes and opinions that he now saw no point in not gratifying: hating luggage, for instance, he chose to keep complete wardrobes in all the places in which he was most likely to spend time – Beverly Hills, New York, and London. In the same way, he adopted expressions and mannerisms very much his own, some leftovers from movie parts, some purely idiosyncratic colloquialisms: 'Fat chance department' or 'FCD', he would say down the phone to friends, when he considered some proposal they were putting to him absurd, or 'You said it, I didn't' to reporters who made remarks they wanted Grant to confirm.

He was helped in almost everything he now chose to do by his remarkable health and stamina. Grant, Weaver came to see during the many years of their association, was quite simply never ill. Nor did he seem to suffer from the palest traces of jet-lag, showing exceptional resilience after long flights across the Atlantic and eager, always, to make plans rather than go to bed to rest and adapt to the change in hour.

In time, the intense and obsessively cloistered life of a recluse in Beverly Grove Drive gave way to a more reasonable pattern, of occasional outings, outside interests, and renewed contacts with old friends, even if these always took place away from his own house. He went to dinner with Danny Kaye, with whom he shared a birthday, and who cooked him the Chinese food he so much enjoyed; he lunched at the Polo Lounge with Mervyn Le Roy, the producer and director, who made him a director of the California Race Track, and, as Jennifer grew older, he took her to baseball games and even to rock concerts, which he would attend as nearly incognito as he could manage, his hat pulled as far forward over his face as he could put it and still be able to see something of the stage. One of Grant's more surprising enthusiasms was for magic and magicians; in Los Angeles there exists a private club where the world's most famous entertainers are invited to perform, and here Grant became a regular visitor, dining in the club, and wandering around watching the card and coin tricks. On the occasion of one of Prince Philip's visits to California, it was to the Magic Castle that Grant, in his capacity as exile host, took him for the evening.

Privately, however, Grant remained a sober and slightly fastidious man, with no taste for the extravagances and crudeness of some of Hollywood's more outrageous or flamboyant spectacles. Of the Friar's Club, a gathering of people from the movie world who on joining assume titles taken from the monastic orders – abbot, friar – and amuse themselves in 'Roasts' at which new members are vilified and lambasted, all in fun, Grant once complained to McIntosh: 'It's not my cup of tea . . . it's so ribald. It is really so, well, ugh . . . I just didn't want anything to do with it . . . Listening to a lot of dirty jokes.'

What did not ease with the passing of time, on the other hand, was Grant's hatred for crowds and publicity. He grew more adept at handling pestering or offensive strangers, and devised his own way of dealing with autograph hunters, either by refusing them altogether, on the very reasonable grounds that their request would undoubtedly precipitate an onslaught of other autograph hunters, or asking them to wait and be discreet so that he could sign their book surreptitiously when he was sure no one was looking. But he has never lost a sense of panic in vast crowds – hardly surprising perhaps when he is liable to emerge from them without buttons or glasses and handkerchiefs. Grant is in fact probably the only living movie actor for whom Bloomingdales, the famous New York department store, has consented to open, so that he could shop alone, unmolested by crowds, at a moment when the store was shut to the general public.

This compulsive terror of publicity and the limelight has

continued all his life to torment him. All the more so, as the fascination he has exercised on succeeding generations of Americans never appears to abate. In a land where there is no royalty, stars are royal. And Grant is more royal than anyone, a fact he acknowledges, with a show of modesty combined with a great deal of genuine reluctance. Even his own Lifetime Award, presented to him at the Kennedy Center when he was seventy-seven, to the strains of the theme song from *Charade*, the movie in which he had starred with Audrey Hepburn, filled him more with anguish than apparent happiness, though he handled the presentation with his customary throw-away lines and expressions of profound self-deprecation: 'As a rule,' he told the assembled crowds, after a touching tribute from Audrey Hepburn, 'I have tended to avoid these events. I rarely go because I'm terrible at making speeches. The thought of that duty leaves me feeling helpless. Jimmy Stewart, on the other hand, seems to like them. Perhaps Jimmy should represent us all the time.' After the laughter he went on: 'I was told by someone that Helen Hayes [another award winner] said it would be high time to get off the tribute circuit and back to work after the evening at the Kennedy Center. I liked that, the tribute circuit. The difference is that the Kennedy Center event is the only one of its kind. I'm glad to be part of it.' Tributes or no tributes, Grant had no intention of getting back into the movie business. He continued occasionally to read scripts. But no bait was appealing enough to lure him out of retirement.

More surprising, perhaps, was that even with the leisure that came when Grant left the screen, he never seemed to want to take any hand in shaping the fortunes of the industry itself. Other stars have retired into roles of advisers, presidents of film guilds, spokesmen for the politics of the movie world and for Hollywood. That life held no appeal for Grant: he had been an actor, and his days as an actor were now over. There was no other part for him to play in Hollywood. To McIntosh, he sometimes gave the impression of a man rationing his name and his time, with a caution that owed something to natural shyness, but also to a canny awareness of the heightened value that rarity confers. Thus, he

150

would take part in a radiothon for the Leukemia Foundation talking on live radio with a doctor and asking the sort of questions any anxious parent might ask, appear at a benefit at the Houston Astrodome to help widows and children of the astronauts who had died in a fire on the launch-pad of one of the Apollo launchings, and read the nativity every Christmas at one of the Disneylands, in memory of his friendship with Walt Disney, but he would not lend his name to anything he deemed over-commercial, frivolous, or vulgar.

When it came to politics, Grant was just as detached. While other Hollywood celebrities have endorsed presidents and lent their names to causes, Grant remained a strangely remote observer of world events. A lifelong acquaintance of the Reagans from Ronald Reagan's movie days, he seemed a natural supporter when the actor stood for president. And yet he would say of himself that he did not always vote on the same ticket, and offended the Reagans greatly when he chose unexpectedly to introduce Mrs Ford rather than Mrs Reagan at one Californian political rally.

As the 1970s drew to a close, so Grant seemed to his friends to be beginning at last to slow down. Lord Mountbatten's murder appeared to affect him particularly. After his funeral, he rang McIntosh, sounding depressed and weary: 'I'm absolutely pooped, and I'm so goddamned old,' he announced, with a new note of defeat in his voice. 'I'm due to go to Taiwan at the end of October . . . every son of a gun wants me on their goddamn dais. I'm going to quit all next year. I'm going to lie in bed . . . I shall just close all doors, turn off the telephone, and enjoy my life.' Not, perhaps, all that remarkable a desire for a man nearing eighty.

Inevitably, in Grant's case, the pessimism was both misplaced and extremely short lived. The next phone call was on a very different key. McIntosh had rung to tell Grant that he was leaving for Europe and to ask whether there was anything he could do for him in England. This time Grant's voice was ebullient: 'There's a dear, dear girl there whom I adore. She's so helpful. . . A very, very attractive girl.'

The girl's name was Barbara Harris. She was English and she

worked in the public relations department of the Royal Lancaster Hotel. By March 1979, Grant was reporting frantically to McIntosh: 'They know who she is. My God – there's been a million photographers chasing us every day.' Cary Grant had found a new leading lady.

Barbara Harris was destined for Grant's private life, not a return to the movies. In April 1981 they got married, naturally in the greatest secrecy, and announced it two weeks later at the Palm Springs home of Frank Sinatra. All the old vitality was back, with trips planned and made, to Hong Kong, Monte Carlo, London, Madrid, and Barcelona.

11

Without Reservations

Perhaps Grace Kelly put it best. 'Everyone grows older,' the late Princess Grace of Monaco once said, 'except Cary Grant.'

Following his 1981 marriage to Barbara Harris, Princess Grace's assessment of Grant's agelessness seemed accurate to most people. In the eyes of media commentators and the general public alike, Grant's full shock of white hair, his now-permanent, oversized, horn-rimmed glasses, and the deepening lines on that ever-tanned face, were not evidence of age or infirmity, but props attending Cary Grant's latest role – the last real movie star.

But Grant himself was aware that the final credits were rolling on the horizon. In the mid-1970s, he had said: 'I doubt if I have more than 70,000 hours left, and I'm not about to waste any of them.' With the help of his last marriage, and his love for his daughter, Grant made good that resolve to reap the highest dividends possible from those remaining hours.

The bond between himself and Barbara seemed the fulfilment of a yearning that had been Grant's all his life. During the five-and-a-half years of their marriage, and before, Barbara became all things to her husband. More than a wife, she was also his companion, executor, friend, and assistant, as well as an elixir of love and youth. In response to his love for her, she prepared favourite meals for him, chauffered him about Hollywood, screened his telephone calls, dickered and dealt with the builders on their Beverly Hills home, and, figuratively and literally, was his mainstay behind the scenes and in public.

Dyan Cannon had complained that Grant was a difficult, even domineering, husband. Not so Barbara. She seemed to have tuned-in to his emotional and intellectual frequencies better than had any of his previous wives, or the many women with whom his magic name had been linked romantically.

Of her husband, Barbara Harris Grant said, 'He is a complex man, extremely kind and intelligent. He has a wonderful humour in him. I think sometimes when people are dominating, it is out of shyness or not feeling at ease in a situation.'

Recently, Lesley Harris, Barbara's mother, confirmed the accounts of Grant's happy alliance with her daughter. In December 1986, at her home in England, Mrs Harris said, 'They visited me every summer. Cary always came over for the Wimbledon tennis tournament and dropped in here. They visited me in July,' she continued, 'and were more affectionate than ever. Cary was very open about showing his feelings toward Barbara. You could see the adoration in his eyes. They didn't hug or hold hands, the way a couple of schoolkids might do. But their happiness in each other showed clearly in the looks they shared.'

Finally, Mrs Harris summarized the relationship between her daughter and Grant, saying: 'Both of them had a keen sense of humour. I think that's what first drew them to each other and that's what kept them so close.'

Barbara Grant herself has been admirably candid in revealing her feelings about their years of courtship and her marriage to Grant. In a 1985 interview for *Parade* with author and journalist Cleveland Amory, at the Grant's Beverly Hills home, she was asked about her knowledge of Grant before they met in London. 'I had heard about him, of course,' she said. 'But I was born and grew up in Tanganyika [Tanzania], so I hadn't seen many of his movies – now I've seen all of them. When I first came to California, I really had no idea of marrying Cary. I was simply terrified of our age difference. But we decided we could live with each other. When I told my mother I was going to marry Cary, all she said was, "If it makes you happy, it makes me happy". She's a good mum.

'We got married out there,' Barbara told Amory, nodding

154

towards the terrace of their home. 'Cary found out that, in California, a couple who have been living together for three years don't need a marriage licence, and that appealed to him. There were just the four of us – Cary and me, and Jennifer and the judge. We didn't tell anybody for two weeks, but then we went to the Sinatras at Palm Springs, and there were a lot of married people there, so we told them. Once you tell anybody out here anything, everybody knows it by the next day.'

Revealing his marriage at so conspicuous a setting as Frank Sinatra's Palm Springs house was a privilege Grant had earned. During more than a half-century of stardom and celebrity, Cary Grant moved in stellar circles, becoming identified with all that is charming and elegant. That Grant, the ultimate standard of romance and fame, should choose a gathering of his peers like Sinatra at which to reveal his latest marriage seems no less than appropriate.

In their years together, the Grants kept up warm social contacts with such superstars as Sinatra, Burt Reynolds, and Gregory Peck, as well as with President and Mrs Reagan and Prince Rainier. Appearing at resplendent public affairs, like the November 1986 Hollywood party honouring Clint Eastwood, was also on their social calendar. But by and large, Cary and Barbara Grant lived a simple, intimate married life. In the morning, Grant usually attended to business – placing phone calls and writing letters. Afternoons often found him at baseball games – he was an avid fan of the Los Angeles Dodgers – or at Hollywood Park for the horse races. Most of the time, though, the Grants stayed at home. He read or rested, reportedly lounging in the comfortable cotton kaftan Barbara made for him, or swam in their pool. In the evenings, they might play parlour games, or sit watching television with their two cats, E.Q. and Sausage.

Not that Barbara was reduced to hand-holding domesticity hidden in her husband's shadow. That would have been out of character for her. Barbara was the youngest daughter of a British Provincial Commissioner, James Harris, and spent most of her childhood in Dar-Es-Salaam, Tanzania. From the age of ten, she was educated in England. After attending secretarial school in London, she held a variety of secretarial and semi-executive positions before pulling down the public relations job at the Royal Lancaster Hotel.

That experience, added to the unique exposure that marriage to Cary Grant gave her, made Barbara Harris a natural for such part-time projects as hosting designer fashion shows, or working with the Princess Grace Foundation.

Barbara also worked with Penney's, an American department store chain, work she was pragmatic about. At an exclusive 1983 showing of designer Halston's creations for Penney's, in Houston, Texas, Barbara said, 'If I were just Barbara Harris and not married to Cary Grant, I don't think I would have been asked.' Typically, she may have underestimated her personal value in such endeavours. A Penney's spokesman explained that the company had enlisted Barbara for the fashion work because she 'typifies the new woman who appreciates fashionable designs at a believable price'. Designer Halston went further, remarking, 'I think Barbara has style and panache'.

Of course, Jennifer continued to play a central role in Grant's life after his marriage to Barbara, and frequently spent week-ends in Los Angeles with Cary and Barbara, away from her classes at Stanford University in Palo Alto, California. Described widely as a beautiful, confident, and polished young woman, Jennifer's college friends have testified to her unpretentiousness and warm manner.

Of his daughter, Grant said in the December 1986 issue of *People*, 'she is my greatest production'. He went on to say, 'She's the most winsome, captivating girl I've ever known, and I've known quite a few. We have an honest relationship. We level with each other. I know when she's looking at me she's not thinking, "I wonder if I can get this old goat for a BMW".'

Grant's relationship with his daughter was one of the supreme sources of his overall happiness in his mature years. Jennifer's understanding and endorsement of his relationship with Barbara were, in fact, paramount in making the marriage a success. That Jennifer might have resented another woman coming into Grant's life would have been understandable. Jennifer's opposition to a Cary–Barbara union could have made a difference, a cause for anxiety for Barbara prior to their marriage in April 1981.

'The hardest part for me,' Barbara said, speaking of that potential hurdle in the Cleveland Amory interview in *Parade*, 'was meeting Jennifer for the first time. I think it's the most difficult thing I've ever had to go through. I knew how Cary felt about her, and I wanted so much for her to like me. I was actually terrified. We're such good friends now that it seems dumb, thinking back. Cary asked Jennifer if she'd mind if he married me.'

Grant confirmed asking for Jennifer's approval to marry Barbara. 'Look,' he confessed saying to his then fifteen-year-old daughter, according to the December *Star*, 'How would you feel if I asked Barbara to marry me? I'm getting on. I need her.'

Jennifer is reported to have responded with tears of joy. Her subsequent support and heartfelt warmth towards her father and his new wife are tributes to Jennifer Grant's precocious maturity and deep sensitivity.

Adopting the homebody role in the 1980s did not mean reclusivity for Cary Grant, by any means. He continued on the boards of Fabergé, MGM, Western Airlines, and a number of other major businesses. During the years of Ronald Reagan's presidency, Grant was several times a guest at White House state dinners. In October 1984, Grant's presence was *de rigeur* when MGM celebrated its sixtieth anniversary by formally dedicating the Cary Grant Theatre on its studio lot. Having made five of his movies at MGM, Grant was presented with a ten-inch gold lion with diamond eyes, from Cartier – a symbol of the studio's trade mark. That evening climaxed with a black-tie dinner-dance for 500 top Hollywood celebrity guests, guarded by two 750-pound ice sculptures of Leo the Lion, held on MGM's Stage 27.

The 1981 Kennedy Center honours ceremony in Washington, D.C., which celebrates the achievements of America's leading performing artists, may have inspired one of Grant's most popular continuing public performances in his last years – the touring

157

one-man show called 'A Conversation with Cary Grant'.

According to William S. Paley, founder and long-time chairman of the Columbia Broadcasting System [CBS], one of America's leading commercial television and radio broadcasting corporations, he suggested to his friend Grant, after the Kennedy Center event, that he come to New York City for a similar tribute. Grant agreed, and Paley put together a benefit programme for the Museum of Modern Art, which was finally held on 27 June, 1984.

Paley sent out letters to a select list of 200 of New York's wealthiest and most prominent personalities. All 200 invitees accepted. In formal gowns and black ties the New Yorkers gathered, with names like Rockefeller, Whitney, and Vanderbilt; the fashion designer Ralph Lauren; *Cosmopolitan* magazine's publisher-editor, Helen Gurley Brown; and many more. As the *New York Times* quipped, 'Just the usual group of Cary Grant fans'.

The evening consisted of a cocktail party, a viewing of excerpts of some of Grant's films, and a dinner in tribute to Grant and his film career, and it netted $200,000 for the MOMA'S annual fund.

Following the film clips, Grant fielded questions about his career. According to the *New York Times* account of that glittering evening, Grant charmed his audience with a witty, self-effacing style reflecting the urbane image he had for so long honed into a work of stage and movie artistry.

'It's always difficult to answer questions about my career,' Grant told his admirers that night, 'but it will be especially hard with such an erudite audience.' Winking, he added, 'There are always a few opening ploys people use whenever they ask me questions. The first is: Why I didn't receive an Oscar for any of my roles? Well, no one voted for me, of course. But I don't carry any grudges. The second is: What is my favourite movie? Well, I don't have one. People tend to look at older antiques, including movies, with a special reverence. But I don't think antiques are any better because they're antiques.

'The third ploy,' Grant went on, 'is: Who was my favourite leading lady? Well, I don't have one of those either. Of course, I made more movies with some leading actresses than with others. Like Kate Hepburn, for instance. Now, Kate's a great girl.'

His receptions at the Kennedy Center tribute and the Museum of Modern Art demonstrated to Grant that his name and his image were golden assets. The success of those evenings almost certainly gave him the seed from which the 'Conversations' series arose. Having discovered the magnetic attraction that his legendary status held for Americans of all ages and backgrounds, Grant moved all across the United States with his one-man show. Appearing in such unglamorous communities as Texarkana, Texas, Joliet, Illinois, or Stamford, Connecticut, Grant played to packed, adulatory houses, wherever he went, usually raising money for charitable causes.

According to the *Star* publication, when once asked why he continued such a strenuous endeavour, Grant answered: 'I want my wife to see this country. I want Barbara to know every fascinating corner of the United States. Touring with my show, with Barbara at my side, is the best way I can think of managing that.'

Observers reported that Grant busied himself with every detail of his show, telling projectionists just when to run designated movie clips, and even checking the placement of microphones into which the audience members would speak their questions from the floor. The pace was hectic and taxing, but Grant seemed determined to give his audiences all that they expected, and to show Barbara, forty-seven years his junior, that her husband was more than a doddering octogenarian.

On two separate occasions, Grant took his show to the La Mirada Civic Theatre in Orange County, California, near Los Angeles. A sample of his remarks to the crowd in the 1,264-seat house during his 1985 appearance there is instructive about the later Cary Grant: updating his opinion on his favourite actress, Grant revealed that, 'with all due respect to dear Ingrid [Bergman]', he had preferred Grace Kelly as a co-star, saying she had 'serenity'; asked if he had a nutritional secret for staying so fit, Grant said, 'No, not a damn thing. I just breathe in . . . and out . . . I don't smoke . . . do everything in moderation. Except making love'; did he plan to make any more movies? 'Put that in your "fat-chance" department,' he said, according to the *Los Angeles Times*. But he added that he did get a boost from his occasional one-man appearances in places like the La Mirada Theatre. Earlier, he had termed such performances, 'ego-fodder'.

That evening also demonstrated the appeal Grant had for so many people. An elderly woman in a wheelchair had come to the civic theatre from a nursing home nearby. Though cameras and tape-recorders were banned from Grant's appearances, the disabled woman raised her hand and asked if she could take Grant's picture to show to her fellow nursing-home patients.

According to the *Los Angeles Times*, Grant asked her, 'Won't they believe you were here?'

'But they may not believe *you* were here,' she replied.

With typical Grant class, he declined to be photographed, but invited the woman to come down and say hello. She was the only one in the audience that evening who got to touch Cary Grant.

In February 1986, Grant made another appearance at the La Mirada. The *Los Angeles Times* reported that the audience again covered all ages, both sexes, and all backgrounds.

> Although there had been almost no publicity, it was a packed house. An attractive blond in a white fur stood near the sold-out notice on the box-office window waving her 'I need two tickets' sign. She got them and rushed to let her mother know they were getting in as another woman grabbed the discarded sign to begin her own search.
>
> A 14-year-old girl came with her parents and grandparents to tell Grant that she and her friend loved his movies. One woman got her ticket for her 30th birthday. A man came to tell the star that he had seen him when Grant gave a similar performance 43 years ago at an Army camp.

Again, the subject of Grant's fitness came up. While he urged his audience to take care of their health and enjoy life, he poked fun at himself, saying, 'I'm a fake. Watch me waddle off stage. And catch me going upstairs sometime.'

The success of the Grant appearances took a toll, however, and Grant's eighty-plus years were making themselves felt. In October 1984, Grant had suffered a mild stroke. At the time, his doctors warned him to slow down, but he maintained the same fast-paced lifestyle.

He was never oblivious to the possibility of his own demise, however. 'I don't know how I consider death,' he told a *Washington Post* reporter in a 1983 interview, when asked about dying. 'So many of my friends have been doing it recently,' he added, ticking-off the names of Grace Kelly, Ingrid Bergman, and David Niven. 'My only fear is that I don't embarrass others. That I don't die an ugly death. I hope I do it well. My mother did it rather well. She just went to sleep. That's what I'd like to do. Who knows? I may go outside and get knocked down by a cab.'

Many would say, with sincere reverence, that Grant did do it well.

He and Barbara arrived in Davenport, Iowa, on Friday, 28 November 1986, to do a scheduled 'Conversation' the next night. They checked into Davenport's Blackhawk Hotel. The next day they were given a tour of the city by a local businessman, who had helped to arrange Grant's appearance. At about 3 p.m., Grant felt sick and is said to have vomited several times. No one became alarmed, however, thinking that the eighty-two-year-old star merely had an upset stomach.

At 4 p.m., Grant arrived at Davenport's Adler Theatre to rehearse his show. Some present noticed that he was having increased problems as the rehearsal progressed, stumbling on stage, appearing confused at times.

By 5 p.m., Grant complained of not feeling well, and was helped by Barbara into his dressing-room. He refused suggestions that a doctor be called.

Grant stayed in the dressing-room, hoping to recover, until 6 p.m., when he was placed in a wheelchair and rolled to a car to go back to the Blackhawk Hotel. In his hotel room, Grant's condition worsened, and Barbara called the Adler Theatre to cancel the evening's show.

At 7.45 p.m., reportedly against Grant's wishes, a doctor was called. The cardiologist arrived and took up the effort to get Grant to a hospital. Again, he refused, insisting that he only needed to rest.

By 9 p.m., Barbara and the doctors took matters into their own hands. Within fifteen minutes, they had Grant in the emergency room of nearby St Luke's Hospital. A CAT scan revealed that he had suffered a massive stroke. A paramedic who attended Grant as Barbara accompanied him to the hospital in the back of an ambulance, said that Grant's last words, addressed to his wife, were: 'I love you, Barbara . . . don't worry.'

At 11.22 p.m. Central Standard Time, on the night of 29 November 1986, Cary Grant was pronounced dead by the doctors at St Luke's Hospital in Davenport, Iowa.

Ironically, the doctors also claim that, had he entered a hospital earlier, Grant might have survived.

Initially shaken by her husband's death, Barbara drew upon her innate reserves of strength, composed herself, and executed her first duties as Cary Grant's widow. Going to a telephone, she called Jennifer in California to tell the twenty-year-old Stanford student of her father's death. Next, Barbara placed a call to her own mother in England. At 2.45 a.m., she boarded a chartered Lear jet to accompany her husband's body back to Los Angeles.

News of Grant's death flashed around the world. Universally, the tributes from those who had known Grant, worked with him, or followed his career, were laudatory and superlative. Perhaps one of the most penetrating and comprehensive tributes was paid by Broadway stage and movie actress Alexis Smith, who played opposite Grant as Mrs Cole Porter in the 1946 biographical film *Night and Day*. She said: 'I think that maybe he was the best movie actor that ever was. As opposed to being this monumental star . . . he was really a very serious actor. The problems of the actor came before that of the star. I just think . . . it's quite wonderful to live as obviously rich and full a life as he did and to still be at the peak of energy, health, and vitality and attractiveness.'

In a stroke of irony, the Sunday night following Grant's death, the CBS television network had scheduled the showing of the

pre-filmed Variety Club Clint Eastwood Tribute, at which Grant
read a congratulatory message from President Reagan to actor
Eastwood. For most of his multitude of fans, that television
programme would be their last glimpse of the beloved and admired
Grant.

According to Grant's will, dated 26 November 1984, his body
was to be cremated and no funeral service was to be held. The will,
in itself, offers an intriguing insight into the star's mind and
character. A thorough businessman as well as an actor and
showman, Grant ensured that his will was a detailed and careful
document that covered many eventualities. From a frugal childhood and the hardships of his earlier show business career, Grant
had learned the value of a dollar or a pound. Though he could be
generous and thoughtful, Grant's tightness was legendary. He was
said even to remove the buttons from shirts he was planning to
discard. ('The buttons are all right,' he would say, 'it's the shirts that
are no good.')

By the provisions of his will, the Grant estate was meticulously
divided. To his wife Barbara, Grant bequeathed their Beverly Hills
home, all its contents, his works of art, and his automobiles. He also
stated that half his after-tax financial wealth, in addition to specific
bequests, should go to Barbara, and the other half to a trust fund for
his daughter Jennifer.

His clothing, jewellery, and other personal effects were to be
divided by his attorney, Stanley Fox, among relatives and close
friends. Specifically named as recipients were Frank Sinatra, MGM
boss Kirk Kerkorian, movie producer Stanley Donen, and *Los
Angeles Times* film critic Roderick Mann.

To his bookkeeper, Grant left $100,000, and $10,000 apiece was
to go to the son and the granddaughter of his attorney. Remembering his British origins, he also left money to Margaret Leach, the
widow of his deceased cousin Eric. Finally, to the John Tracy Clinic
for the hearing-impaired, Grant bequeathed $20,000.

Leaving nothing to chance, Grant concluded his will with the
threat that any beneficiary 'directly or indirectly' contesting or
attacking the will would automatically lose his or her share. Cary

Grant is reputed to have left a fortune valued at $60 million.

In the years after Grant's retirement from films, much was written analysing and interpreting his career and his significance to modern culture. His death will doubtless spur more critical consideration of his work, and no future examination of mid-twentieth-century popular entertainment will be complete without some examination of the Cary Grant phenomenon.

But perhaps the final authority on that phenomenon must be Grant himself. Fortunately for us, over the years, he occasionally reflected on his artistry and his image, and his remarks are integral to the public record.

Of himself, Grant said, 'When I see an old clip, I sometimes wonder if that was really me in that scene. I never understood what people found interesting in me. I pretended to be somebody I wanted to be, until, finally, I became that person. Or he became me. Or we met at some point. It's a relationship.'

Again, in a famous quote, Grant said, 'Everybody wants to be Cary Grant. I want to be Cary Grant.'

But in summary of his whole life – first, as Archie Leach, lonely child, acrobat, travelling trouper, stage actor; and then as Cary Grant – at the time of his informal retirement from films, he articulated perhaps the best judgement, saying 'I'm filled with things I want to do and now things are coming along every day. Why, I've got to live to be 400 to do all the things I've got to do. But even if I don't live that long – even if I die soon – it's been a wonderful life.'

Index

Index

Index

Index

Vanderbilt, 158
Vincent, Frank, 41

Walk Don't Run, 51, 52, 53, 55, 97
Warner, Jack, 97
Warners Studios, 43
Warwick Hotel, New York:
 penthouse, 104–6
war work: whistle-stop tour, 39
Washington Post, 161
Weaver, David, 68, 70–1, 85–6, 130
Weaver, William (Bill); background,
 52; becomes Grant's secretary, 52–
 3; work routine, 53, 55–6; meets
 Dyan Cannon, 54–5; helps choose
 Dyan's clothes, 59; demands made
 on, 59–60; voyage with Grant on
 Oriana, 61–2; accompanies Grant
 to see Jennifer, 63–4; skills as
 childminder, 68; looks after
 Jennifer, 70–1; finds horse for
 Jennifer, 71; deals with derelict

house, 80–6; tree-felling mishap,
 85–6; rises early, 86; alarmed by
 Grant's eccentricities, 92; travels in
 plane with Grant, 103; paid by
 Fabergé, 106–7; security problems
 in Las Vegas, 113–14; accompanies
 Mountbatten, 114–15; involved
 with Grant's women, 15, 125–6,
 130–2; holiday in France, 129; at
 Special Oscar presentation, 14, 17;
 Grant's role of mentor to, 139
Welch, Raquel, 113, 114, 126, 135
Wells, Rose, 103
Wenke, Judge Robert A., 67
West, Mae, 36, 45, 145
Western Airlines, 111–12, 128, 157
White House, 157
Whitney, 158
Winchester, Jane Ellen, 79
woodpecker: chasing out of house,
 55–6
Wray, Fay, 32, 36

171